Charity & Ted Bradshaw

STAYING
I DO

COMMITTED, CONNECTED &
CRAZY IN LOVE
FOR A LIFETIME

This book is not intended to provide medical advice or to take the place of medical advice and treatment from your personal physician. Readers are advised to consult their own doctors or other qualified health professionals regarding the treatment of their medical problems. Neither the publisher nor the authors take any responsibility for any possible consequences from any treatment, action, or application of medicine, supplement, herb, or preparation to any person reading or following the information in this book. If readers are taking prescription medications, they should consult with their physicians and not take themselves off medicines to start supplementation without the proper supervision of a physician.

Staying I Do:
Committed, Connected & Crazy in Love for a Lifetime

www.charitybradshaw.com
www.tedandcharity.com

ISBN: 978-1-64123-279-1
eBook ISBN: 978-1-64123-280-7

Printed in the United States of America
© 2019 by Charity and Ted Bradshaw

Whitaker House
1030 Hunt Valley Circle
New Kensington, PA 15068
www.whitakerhouse.com

Library of Congress Cataloging-in-Publication Data (Pending)

1 2 3 4 5 6 7 8 9 10 11 ᴜᴜ 26 25 24 23 22 21 20 19

Dedication

To Luke, Kate, Natalie, and Presley—
four of the best reasons why we continue to grow our love
and invest in our marriage.

Preface

Saying "I do" is one of the most exciting moments in a person's life. For brides, it is usually preceded by putting on the perfect dress, shoes, and veil, coupled with the skills of a hair and makeup team with magical powers used to turn them into a real-life princess. For grooms, it's the tux, some hair products, and probably a round of golf because let's face it, guys can be ready in about six minutes.

These days, when a couple gets engaged, nearly all of their planning is devoted to the wedding and reception. Months of work and thousands of dollars are spent preparing for a three-hour event. But what about the marriage—you know, the stuff that happens once the DJ turns the music off, the bouquets wilt, and the last suitcase has been unpacked from the honeymoon? Real life. Married life.

When we were expecting our first child, we noticed there were many books dedicated to what was happening during the pregnancy, but very few helping you figure out, step by step, what to do once that baby made its entrance into the world.

WHAT ABOUT AFTER THE VOWS?

The same is true for marriage. There are books and magazines dedicated to helping you pick out the perfect playlist, color scheme, and refreshments for your wedding and reception, but what about navigating the first fight that actually shakes the foundation of your relationship? Or dealing with family members who repeatedly ask for money? Or when tragedy strikes and you both handle the situation differently? These scenarios aren't necessarily top of mind early on; they often sneak up on us and then lower the boom.

Staying I Do is a collection of conversations, experiences, and observations purposefully and prayerfully compiled to help support and encourage couples who want to not only stay married for life, but also be *crazy in love* while doing it. We are the type of people who would rather learn from someone else's mistakes and successes—and that is our mission for this book. We have poured our hearts out and pulled back all of the curtains, with the hope and divine expectation of supporting strong, loving, fun, and healthy marriages.

HOLDING ON AND BUILDING TRUST

Here's a real-life example of holding on to someone and learning to trust each other:

Before sending volunteers off on a two-month mission trip, the organizers held some team-building exercises that included a ropes course. Each two-person team would climb a pole until they reached the platform that was about twenty feet above ground. Extending from this platform were two parallel ropes tethered to another platform roughly forty feet away. Each team was supposed to walk on the ropes from one platform to the other. There was nothing to hold on to for balance.

To get across without falling and being caught by the awkward harness system, each person stepped on to a rope opposite their teammate. They faced each other, locked both hands, and leaned in with their full body weight. They then stepped sideways on the ropes to reach the other platform, communicating to time their steps and build their trust in each other. Outside of a few strongly competitive teams, speeding across wasn't the goal. Finishing was.

That ropes course gives us an accurate visualization of marriage. Both team members were equal. Both were necessary. Both had to be strong yet simultaneously dependent. Both had to give their all and be totally accepting of their partner to reach the goal. There were shaky times, real scares, and plenty of laughter, some of it nervous, but the outcome was rewarding.

Marriage is just like this. It's not 50 + 50 = 100 but rather 100 + 100 = 1. On the ropes course, if someone decided to pull back or withhold some of their weight, the other team member lost stability and security. The same thing happens in marriage. If one or both withhold love, approval, appreciation, trust, service, and preference, the marriage loses the delicate balance that comes from both spouses being all in.

Acknowledgments

To Charles and Frances Hunter (aka Poppa and Grandma), thank you for modeling love, service, affirmation, forgiveness, affection, submission, support, and the value of togetherness. Your legacy is one we hope to continue as well as pass on.

To Joan Hunter (aka Mom), thank you for your constant support and persistent nudges to get this book written. Your belief in us is unparalleled. You are the best.

To Darin and Cheryl Newton, thank you for allowing us to witness your beautiful family of seven and how you tackle life while loving each other so deeply. You gave us hope that we could have children and still be wildly in love. Our children thank you, too!

Contents

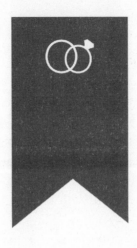

Introduction

We wrote this book for:

ENGAGED OR NEWLYWED COUPLES

For those of you reading who are in the early stages of marriage or even still engaged, our intention for you is that this book will prompt healthy conversations in times of peace when you can think clearly and establish your plans together rather than be reactive when the trying moments arise. So much pain can be avoided by talking through tough things before they are actually a problem. Imagine building your marriage the right way from the start by investing in knowing your spouse's values, boundaries, hopes, and fears, so you can grow together. Imagine how empowering it will be when you give and receive total honesty, commitment, and trust.

7-YEAR-ITCH OR BURIED-IN-PARENTING COUPLES

Maybe things were hot and fiery before, but has marriage lost its luster? Does married life feel like a roommate situation with some joint child-rearing responsibilities rather than warm and affectionate, genuinely concerned for one another, and overflowing with sexual intimacy? There probably hasn't been one big major offense, but likely a series of little things that have caused the fire to fade. All is not lost. Our prayer for you is that together, we can help reignite the passion, deepen the connection, and rebuild areas that have been damaged over the years with one of the main focuses being on how to *stay "I do"* amidst busy schedules, parenting responsibilities, and other energy commitments.

EMPTY NESTERS OR MARRIAGE VETERANS

What about you marriage veterans who are years past the wedding ceremony and the house is once again quiet because all of the kids have moved out? Is there still a relationship there or are you strangers who share an address? Have the shifts in identity and roles taken a toll on the heart of your marriage? Loyalty doesn't always equal romance and intimacy. We want to help you remember who you were when you began this lifelong journey, discover who you both are now, and recapture the same love and fascination you had before you said "I do."

NOT EXPERTS, JUST CRAZY IN LOVE

We do not claim to be marriage experts. We are just a crazy-in-love couple willing to talk about things that really happen and offer our opinions on how to shortcut the learning process. In fact, writing a book on marriage has been one of the more intimidating things we've dealt with. It feels like we are putting ourselves in a fishbowl. Our goal is not for you to look at us as standard-setters, but rather allow the points we bring up to foster healthy conversations that lead to positive change.

If you feel your marriage is in need of big changes, let us offer some encouraging words. Big changes are simply a collection of small changes that happen over time. Perhaps you walk away with one small thing you can work on from each chapter. Our belief is when you partner your marriage with God, these small changes will add up and lead to the big changes your heart longs for.

Be Honest

WHERE IT ALL STARTED

Being honest is everything in marriage. It's what separates good from great and average from awesome. It is often one of the hardest things to do, but definitely the one that carries the most benefits. Honesty sets the foundation for trust—and marriages that last are built on trust.

Charity

HONESTY CAME FIRST

Due to my family history, honesty was the first character quality I was looking for in a man. Sure, I wanted to be attracted to him. Yes, it was nice if he had a good job. Above all, however, I had to be able to trust him.

In May 1999, I graduated from Oral Roberts University with a bachelor's degree in music. My idea was to move back home briefly so I could save up money and produce an album just in case my destiny was to become a rock star. To subsidize this epic project, I got a great job at Nordstrom and did very well at it, which only bolstered my chances of getting on the Top-40 chart. I wasn't going to be one of those kids who moves back in and stays. My plans were to move out soon after I paid for the album and live the life. That October, I turned twenty-three. Shortly after that, things started to spiral.

In March 2000, my parents' divorce was finalized after twenty-five years of marriage. I had thought their marriage was so-so, but even that was a lie. The details of my parents' marriage and, ultimately, their divorce, caused me to lose what little faith I had in the confines of marriage.

At the time, I felt like I was the least likely candidate of my circle of friends to get married. I never had a flock of guys chasing me. Well, maybe once. But between being in the friend-zone and being picky, let's just say guys weren't *that* big of a distraction. In May 2001, I was talking to one of my guy-friends who was actually more like the brother I never had. He was living in Nashville with his cool band and they were signed to a label. He suggested I entertain the idea of moving to Nashville for a fresh start. After a few key conversations with family, I agreed to move in January.

I began my six-month exit strategy and savings plan. I was strong and smart and going to do this cross-country adventure on my own. My plan had to be perfect because I was not going to fail in front of everyone or put myself in a position of needing anyone. From what I had seen, that was the definition of marriage for women: needy woman marries strong, dependable man for security and stability, to handle "things she could never do on her own." *Blech!*

Even before I contemplated this move, 2001 was already a very difficult year for me. I didn't realize it, but at the time, I was dealing with depression. What that looked like for me was long stretches of insomnia, fits of crying, and self-destructive choices, like a super-sized helping of clubbing. Mind you, all of this was happening while I was somehow making it to church every Sunday.

Some Sundays were less glamorous than others. To deal with the pain, duplicity, and depression, many times I would have to sit in my car and cry for about fifteen or twenty minutes in between the main service and Sunday school just to be able to cope and not fall apart during the lesson in front of a room full of people.

A VISITOR IN THE CROWD

On Sunday, September 2, 2001, I went to my usual Sunday school class for singles ages twenty-five to thirty-three, which I had done for a while despite the fact I wasn't yet old enough. As a college graduate, the eighteen to twenty-four age group seemed a little too young to me. The church itself had fifteen to seventeen thousand members and our Sunday school classes were correspondingly huge. That Sunday, there were about five hundred singles in the class.

I scanned the room, looking for a place to sit. I couldn't sit beside a familiar face because if they asked me how I was doing, I just knew I would start to cry uncontrollably. Then I spotted a guy I had never seen before who looked like he was highlighted by a spotlight. I decided to sit by him because I thought he was probably a visitor and would keep the conversation nice and shallow. There were about eight of us at that roundtable and during the class, we all engaged in the group questions. Ted said I had some amazing responses that caught his attention, but I couldn't tell you what I said. I was too focused on not crying.

Ted was pretty quiet, but seemed confident. In a somewhat flashy church culture, he stood out as someone who didn't know a thing about appearances. His pants were too short and his Hawaiian print shirt was a bit garish. Later, we found out he was wearing shoes that were way too small. Can you say "intervention"? After the class was over, I hung around and asked Ted some generic questions.

"Where do you work?" I asked. His ocean-blue eyes nearly distracted me from his answer, but I will never forget it.

"I'm a delivery driver for Domino's Pizza."

In a world where many guys might say something like, "I'm a transport agent for a Fortune 500 company," or something else that makes their job sound more glamorous or important, Ted simply told the naked truth. No masks. No games. Just the truth. It was oddly and amazingly attractive.

The next Sunday, I told one of my girlfriends that we needed to look for this guy named Ted. Being the creature of habit he is, I found Ted sitting in the exact same seat. He made me curious about him. He made me want to know more. How could someone be so honest? This may not sound like some big thing to you, but to me, it was everything. I honestly don't remember what happened that Sunday outside of the fact that I wanted to sit by him again and again.

Week after week, we began looking for each other and sitting together. I didn't think too much of it because my move to Nashville was coming up.

HE REMEMBERED

My birthday came six weeks after I met Ted. It was a miracle I even made it to church that Sunday morning because my friends threw me an outrageous party the night before—and they all slept in. Ted's sister had just given birth to her first child, but he came to Sunday school just to wish me happy birthday before going to the hospital to see her. I was blown away that he remembered my birthday considering we barely knew each other.

He said, "I would have gotten you a gift but my friend said it would look like I have the hots for you."

Before I could even think, I spouted off, "And you don't?"

His face turned red. He began stammering and stuttering, trying to figure out how to respond to my awkwardly direct question, making his feelings quite obvious. I did not see this one coming. To give us both a break, I said, "I have to go to the bathroom," and ran off. Once I closed the stall door, I basically freaked out. I was *moving*. I was *not* looking to meet someone, and neither was Ted. In fact, he had told me he started coming to our church because he was looking for male accountability partners.

Eventually, when I came out of the bathroom, Ted was still there. Now, we were both a little red-faced. We smiled, said our goodbyes, and he headed to the hospital. My move to Nashville just got a little more complicated. I was okay leaving my family, my job, my church, and my friends, but a guy was now in the equation. I didn't have time to waste rerouting my life for a *maybe*, nor the energy to go through disappointment. In my mind and in my heart, I felt torn.

FULL DISCLOSURE

Two weeks later, on October 28, 2001, none of my friends showed up for church (again) so I asked Ted if he wanted to go to lunch afterward. I wanted to talk to him and explain why I would soon be moving to Nashville. This was hard because he didn't know me well enough for me to be especially important to him. I felt like I was putting our potential relationship on the line.

The news that I was leaving for Nashville in two months definitely shot his wheels off. I had a feeling this lunch was going to be a defining moment in our relationship—if we were, in fact, going to have one. If he was ever going to be scared away, I was going to make sure it was sooner rather than later. While waiting for our Caesar salads, I proceeded to tell Ted every crazy and awful thing I could think of about me and my family—previous relationship experiences, the details of my parents' divorce, and the "wild" people in my family, not to mention my evangelist grandparents. I knew this was a lot and was prepared for him to thank me for saving us from getting into a relationship we might later regret. However, to my surprise, he basically shrugged and said, "If you think that is bad, wait until you hear about me and my family."

Ted then disclosed many gritty details of his own life, such as his personal debt of over $40,000, his relationship history, being abandoned by his mother as a child, some of his self-destructive choices, and the "wild" members in his own family.

For some reason, everything seemed fine. It was nice that we were both not wasting time pretending to be anything or anyone other than who we really were, quirks and all. In a way, it reminded me of Adam and Eve in the garden, when they were both naked and yet unashamed. (See Genesis 2:25.) Only we were in a restaurant and fully clothed.

Somewhere in the middle of that lunch, the restaurant seemed to get quiet and I heard a voice say, "This is your husband." It wasn't booming or creepy, just matter-of-fact. Keep in mind, I did not have much faith in marriage at this point, yet here was this voice basically telling me I'm going to marry Ted, whom I barely knew. So, as any forward-thinking woman would do, I asked Ted what his last name was. I didn't even know that yet!

"Bradshaw."

Charity Bradshaw. That sounds amazing, I thought. Sold!

Toward the end of our meal, Ted said, "Well, I guess I'll see you next Sunday."

The thought of going an entire week without seeing him was unbearable now that I knew I was going to marry him. At the risk of sounding desperate, forward, or borderline psychotic, I told him the truth.

"I don't think I can wait that long."

"Okay, I will call you later with my schedule."

I went home that afternoon, called two friends, and told them, "I think I just had lunch with the man I'm going to marry."

"Who?"

"Ted."

"Ted who?"

"I know, right?!"

It hit me then that I didn't know much about Ted other than the crazy stuff you tell no one and that he worked for Domino's. But I *did* know he was honest.

When he said he'd call me "later," I expected him to mean guy-terms "later," like calling Thursday to make plans for the weekend. But Monday, I had a voicemail from him detailing every breakfast, lunch, and dinner option he had available for the entire week.

Wow, maybe I didn't scare him off, I thought.

SPEED DATING

That week, we went on two dates. Even though he was not giving me any hard signals that he was as interested as I was, I still called them dates. And that Saturday, we went to my friend's house for movie night. I couldn't wait for my friends to meet him.

As the movie started, Ted and I sat on the couch, leaving enough room for Jesus between us. All I could think about was that I was going to marry him *and* I was moving in less than two months. I didn't have time to wait and see if this was going to go anywhere. I wanted to know if he felt the same. So I reached over to hold his hand. Instantly, Ted jumped up like the couch was on fire, said to the room, "Does anyone want more wine?" and ran to the kitchen.

All I could think was, *How could I be so wrong? Was I misreading everything going on? I thought he liked me as well…but evidently not.* I sat on my side of the couch, enduring the rest of the movie and playing out the conversation we were about to have in my head. After the movie was over, we said our goodbyes and headed out to the car so he could drive me home.

We didn't take more than ten steps out of the apartment before I asked, "Did my holding your hand make you uncomfortable?" I braced myself for the brutal truth.

"Yes, it did."

What in the world? Doesn't he know we are going to get married? Can't he feel it? I tried to fight it, but I began to cry. He opened the car door and I got in.

I decided right then that I couldn't go another moment without finding out exactly how he felt about me. I asked, "Do you like me?"

"What do you mean?"

"Oh, no, you don't get to play like that. You know what I mean. Do you like me?"

He threw down the hammer. "I don't know if you are the love of my life or a sister in the Lord." His exact words.

I was absolutely crushed and confused. Evidently, the voice in the restaurant only spoke to one of us. We arrived at my apartment, said goodnight, and I went inside and cried. I felt like a fool to think that I was going to marry someone who didn't have feelings for me.

It was a long night for both of us. What Ted didn't tell me right away was that on his drive home from my apartment, he reflected on our conversation and heard God ask him, "Could this be your wife?" Ted thought about all of the things he had asked for in a wife starting with "green eyes, creative, independent, and a good friend." He quickly began to see that what he wanted and prayed for was right in front of him.

I still like to remind Ted of how long those six days were between when I knew I was going to marry him and he knew he was going to marry me.

So, there we were, both of us knowing separately in our hearts that we wanted to marry each other. But wasn't it too soon to talk about marriage after only three dates? Probably. So we waited. We went on as many dates as we could because my time in Dallas was coming quickly to close.

THE LONGEST THREE WEEKS

Thanksgiving was right around the corner, so we decided this would be a good opportunity to meet each other's families since they would already be together at various homes in the Dallas-Fort Worth area. The night before Thanksgiving, Ted called to give me a rundown of his family's schedule and his cooking and cleaning plans. He did everything from the all-night turkey cooking to cleaning up after his roommate's cat so I could breathe at the house.

I just could not believe his level of care and concern for me and his family. This was an all-night preparation preceding an all-day progression of meeting relatives. I almost got lost in the details until the conversation took an unexpected turn. We were talking about how he was going to introduce me and what he was going to say.

"I just want you to know that I want you to be my girl, not just my girlfriend."

Wait, what? Is this a proposal? On the phone?

"Would you be my girl?"

I think my voice conveyed my big smile. "Yes, I would love to." It was the easiest and best decision I ever made.

I prepped for meeting his family members like it was the interview of a lifetime. Thankfully, they made me feel at home right away and we had a great time. Just before we pushed off for the next home, Ted's sister told him to make sure he said goodbye to his family before he moved to Tennessee with me. Bless his heart, the thought of moving with me never entered his mind until that moment. I didn't want to ask him to move. I wanted it to be his idea, not me dragging him away from anything. Thankfully, his family helped him see that moving was a good idea.

Next, we arrived at my mom's house, where he met her, my maternal grandparents, my sisters, and a few other relatives. The first thing Ted saw when we walked in was my youngest sister attempting to knee my other sister's boyfriend where it hurts.

In a panic, he asked, "Is she going to do that to me?"

"Maybe."

WHAT DOES GRANDMA SAY?

Outside of my mom and sisters, I couldn't wait for Ted to meet my grandparents, Charles and Frances Hunter. If I ever got married, I wanted a marriage like theirs. They loved each other, they loved being together, and they made it look so fun. More than anything, I wanted my grandparents' blessing on our relationship. I wanted them to meet Ted and tell me, "Yes, he is a good choice."

My grandmother was a wise woman. At dinner, she had the brilliant idea for us to go around the table and say what we were thankful for. She strategically started with me, which meant it would end with Ted. We all shared our thanks and then it was Ted's turn. He stood up, even though no one else had done so, and began by first sharing his thankfulness for salvation. Before he could finish, my grandmother announced, "Yes, you CAN marry my granddaughter." Mind you, we hadn't said anything to anyone. She just knew.

My grandmother, who was an ordained minister, wanted to marry us as soon as possible. She didn't want us to burn for each other. While that probably was a good idea, Ted wasn't ready right away. He mentioned there were some things he wanted to take care of before we went any further. He didn't want to bring his debt into our marriage, especially since I didn't have any. I could tell he felt ashamed of his situation yet determined to take care of it and not put the burden on me.

Knowing how much he owed, I knew at his current job, it would take a year or two *at least* to pay it off. I didn't want to wait that long to get married. I thought that with my brains and our joint effort, we could pay it off faster together. He reluctantly agreed, but still had strong concerns about the pressure I would feel. I'm thankful he didn't wait until after we got married to share the details of his financial situation. His honesty allowed me to marry him with full knowledge of his debt, move forward, and shoulder it with him.

WHAT'S YOUR SECRET?

Maybe the "skeletons in your closet" aren't financial. Maybe they are past relationships or events, or bad habits like sex addiction, drug usage, or anorexia? Perhaps you even had an abortion you hoped to never speak of again. These types of painful truths can reinforce or break down a relationship. If you've ever been in any kind of recovery program or know anyone who has, you may have heard the adage, "You are only as sick as your secrets."

This rings true in relationships as well. When something is secret, it eats away at you and causes you to feel like who you really are isn't worthy of love. But when you share your secrets with your significant other, it gives you confidence in knowing that how they respond to you is based on knowing all of the facts, not just a select few.

> HONESTY IS WHAT ALLOWS LOVE FROM YOUR SPOUSE TO PENETRATE FULLY INTO YOUR HEART.

Sharing all of your secrets doesn't leave room for the mind games that say, *If you only knew who I really am....* Instead, it says, *You know the real me and you love me anyway.* This is when marriage goes from good to great. You transcend the daily grind of all the nice gestures one would do to keep their spouse happy and move into true intimacy, which is knowing and being known. Honesty with your spouse is not only a gift to them, but also a gift to yourself. Honesty is what allows love from your spouse to penetrate fully into your heart.

Charity

THE LANGUAGE OF LOVE

One book that helped us understand each other is Gary Chapman's *The 5 Love Languages*.[1] We learned that one of my

---

1. Gary Chapman, *The 5 Love Languages: The Secret to Love That Lasts* (Chicago: Northfield Publishing, 1992).

primary love languages is words of affirmation. I feel love when I hear positive, loving things from Ted and people in general.

As much as Ted loves me, speaking positive, loving things did not come naturally to him. He had to think about it and make an effort to share words of affirmation. Throughout our marriage, when I needed or desired his love through words, I could either suffer in silence—because who wants to have to ask, right?—or I could be honest with him and say, like I do now, "Tell me some good things." He knows exactly what I mean and can then tell me what he loves about me.

Your mind will try to mess with you when it comes to expressing a deep need. I know for me, my mind would try to convince me I was being selfish or immature and that I should get over it. One of the wisest things I remember my grandparents saying was, "Be honest, even to the portion of a thought." It didn't seem like revelation when I first heard it, but as various situations arose, I could see its value even more. Ted and I agreed full honesty was the only way for us.

Honesty gives you freedom to be yourself. It's the kind of freedom you might feel when walking around your house in your underwear and not caring one bit. There's full transparency and full acceptance.

HONESTY IN STRUGGLES

Since Ted and I committed to be 100 percent honest with each other, this also meant we shared what we were struggling with. That sounds good in theory, but is quite difficult in practice. I remember one day early in our marriage, maybe just after the first-year mark, Ted told me he needed to talk. *This doesn't sound good,* I thought. We sat down on our couch and by the look on his face, I could tell this was probably not going to be a fun conversation.

He began by confirming his love for me and reminding me of our honesty pledge. That made my mind start following rabbit trails to every possible thing he could tell me, which isn't good considering that if life were a video game, I would be level expert at worst-case scenarios. *Did he want a divorce? Did he have an affair? Did he spend a bunch of money? Did he get in a wreck? Did he find out he's sick?* I had plenty of options to work with in the five to ten seconds leading up to my turn to talk.

It wasn't any of those things, thank God. But it was something that took my breath away in that moment. He shared that he was struggling with lust. Again, the gears in my mind started turning. *Am I not attractive to him anymore? What did I do wrong? Is he going to leave me? Who is she? Am I a boring sex partner?* He could tell by the expression on my face and the tears in my eyes how much this truth hurt. It hurt him to tell me, too. But when he reminded me that I was his best friend and the person he promised to be truthful to, it was a gift. It actually made me trust him more.

After the initial sting, I realized what he was saying was that he didn't want to go through that struggle alone. He wanted me to be aware so that I could be actively involved in helping him move past it. It opened up lines of communication on the topic and the door for us to pray about it together. Even now, as I reflect on that conversation, I am grateful for his honesty.

One of the best habits we have in our marriage is sharing all of our feelings, even if they are embarrassing.

IT'S NOT EXCLUSIVE TO MEN

Fast forward eight or so years later. By this point, I had popped out several kids and was trying to get back into some kind of shape. I was going to the gym pretty regularly and noticed a man who seem to have the same workout schedule as mine. You could tell by looking at him that he was dedicated to fitness. He also had a nice smile. Before I knew it, I began looking for him when I walked into the gym, just checking to see if he was there again. I never talked to him, but admired him from a distance.

One day, I finally admitted to myself that I was lusting after this man. It grieved me to realize this was an area I was weak in. I somehow thought lust was a male issue. I was disgusted with myself. I saw something in me that I hated because of what happened to my parents' marriage and how it affected us children. It was very humbling to realize that I was one bad decision away from hurting people I love and potentially repeating what I swore would never happen in my marriage.

I came home from the gym and told Ted that I was struggling with lust, a conversation I never dreamed of having. He listened with grace and forgiveness and prayed with me. On my own, I prayed that somehow my workouts would no longer coincide with that man's schedule and I'm here to tell you, God answered my prayer. I never saw him again.

IT'S NOT TOO LATE TO BE HONEST

Your marriage may not have a long history of honesty, but that doesn't mean it has to stay that way. You can begin changing the culture of your home and your relationship by dropping façades and responding with grace and forgiveness. The delicate balance of honesty is not just in being honest, but in how you respond when your spouse is honest with you.

There will likely come a time when you will need to share a difficult truth, so be gracious when it's your turn to hear it. Remember, your spouse is the person you promised your life to. They are your biggest investment. Honesty is one of the stabilizing forces that will help your marriage not only last but thrive.

SPEAK NOW OR FOREVER EAT THOSE PEAS

Let's take a common scenario. Your spouse worked really hard on a new recipe, set it down in front of you, and waited in anticipation for you take your first bite. You know this is a setup. The acceptable responses are very limited, especially if you haven't been married long. If you loved the dish and thought it was delicious, hooray! Everyone wins. However, if it was less than amazing, what do you do? Do you try to spare their feelings...or do you tell them the truth?

> HONESTY IS STABILIZING FORCE THAT WILL HELP YOUR MARRIAGE NOT ONLY LAST BUT THRIVE.

If you fake enjoying it, be prepared to eat that meal again and again. Truth is neutral. It's the delivery that matters. Yes, you can express appreciation for the work and love that was poured into the meal, but spare yourself and your spouse the pain and agony of saying you liked it when you really didn't.

Ted

THE EXPERIMENTAL KITCHEN

Over the years, our waistlines grew. As we began to search for ways to reduce them, we would experiment with different recipes we found online or in cookbooks. This was like Russian roulette, shooting in the dark, or modern online dating. You never knew what you were going to get.

Charity would search and search for seemingly palatable recipes, purchase the ingredients, prepare and cook the food, and then hold her breath while she made me go in for the first bite. Like many, we were cutting back on bad carbs and looking for real replacements for some of our favorite foods. Like bread, for example.

After scanning recipes and ratings, Charity found what appeared to be the holy grail of low-carb toast. In fact, she told me that one woman's review said she had it every day and looked forward to it. The ingredient list had me concerned, but I was willing to try anything for that crusty goodness I was craving. Charity prepped two servings of this magic concoction and we both drooled as we waited for it to bake.

The smell should have been my initial warning to stay away, but I still had hope because it had the look and feel of toast. We buttered it and felt like kids on Christmas day, ready to unwrap the big gift. I was not wearing my "I'm the Guinea Pig" shirt that day, but my role was clear.

"Try it," she coaxed.

Within seconds, I spit out that foul, crusty thing, straight into the trash can. Imagine how many times I would have had to eat that nasty cardboard if I had acted as if it was awesome or even decent? Yes, there was time and work involved, and Charity and I both had high hopes for this recipe, but no one should have to eat that stuff, *ever*.

Now, we look for recipes together and I make nearly as many meals as she does. We both promise to never eat food that we don't like and we keep searching for new favorites. It's rewarding to know that I will always know where my food stands with her and vice versa. We will either enjoy or despise our concoctions together.

A WARNING TO THOSE STILL DATING

It is a dangerous path to fake enjoyment of something while dating and then flip once you're married. An example of this we see a lot is when a woman pretends to enjoy watching sports on TV with her man or even watching him play video games when they are dating, but then becomes an infuriated maniac after the wedding.

> WHAT YOU ACCEPT, TOLERATE, AND PARTICIPATE IN WHILE DATING SHOULD BE WHAT YOU PLAN TO LIVE WITH IN MARRIAGE.

You can't expect your spouse to change behavior you have tolerated or pretended to support. Withholding the truth is the same as lying, so be who you are from the very beginning, especially while dating. What you accept, tolerate, and participate in while dating should be what you plan to live with in marriage.

Charity

KNOW YOUR DEAL-BREAKERS

I remember casually hanging out with a guy friend who loved World Wrestling Entertainment. I knew then, just as much as I know now, that I could not spend any of my life watching WWE and that if we were to go any further in our relationship, it was going to be a problem. Being honest with myself allowed me to completely shut down any feelings for him beyond friendship.

IF IT WAS OK THEN, IT'S OK NOW

It is not fair to run this kind of trick play where in one season of your life it's fine and the next, it's over. Right from the start, express what you love, what you don't love, what you enjoy, what you hate, what drives you bonkers, and what makes life amazing.

Many couples have a hard time transitioning from dating because so much faking was going on. Maybe he opened the door for you every time? Maybe you wore makeup whenever he was around? Perhaps one of you faked smiles at the parents' house while listening to them pontificate?

We've seen couples date and then when things start to get serious, all of a sudden, the tattoos are a problem, the motorcycle's a problem, how much they drink is a problem, hanging out with their friends is a problem, spending is a problem, and the list goes on. These issues were there the whole time, yet something changed. If you have a problem with one of their habits, deal with it now, while you're dating. Once you're married, it is part of what you have accepted and agreed to.

Marriage isn't the ultimate do-it-yourself project where you rehab someone and make them over exactly the way you want them. It is about improving together, growing together, learning together, and loving together. Yes, there is plenty of opportunity to encourage growth and greater maturity over time, but you had better expect to do some changing as well. Faking acceptance of things you don't really accept only delays what you want out of the relationship.

Ted

FOUR-STAR FOURTH ANNIVERSARY

For our fourth anniversary, we were living in Nashville, but craving Mediterranean food like we had back in Dallas from our favorite restaurant. I searched and found a place where we could have a nice meal; they even had an "anniversary package." Our firstborn, Luke, was almost a year old, so this dinner out was a real treat. We dressed up, hired a babysitter, and drove to this new and exciting restaurant. The anticipation of this anniversary experience was palpable.

Once we arrived, the hostess greeted us and we were taken to our "special table," which looked very normal up close. I told the server that it was our anniversary and we were supposed to get the anniversary package. Since he was not sure exactly what that meant, he asked for some clarification. The restaurant manager came over and sprinkled a few tiny, metallic stars on our table. "There you go," he said. "Happy anniversary."

Charity and I were extremely underwhelmed with their version of an anniversary package, but we both kept smiling. We wanted each other to think this was the best night ever. It wasn't until the car ride home that we actually opened up about how ridiculous the whole thing was and how disappointed we were.

We laugh about it now because in hindsight, it's really funny, but if we had not been honest, we probably would have spent more time in misery than necessary. If I thought Charity had a great time there, we would have gone back again and again.

When you're married, make a commitment to each other that you won't fake anything. This is not carte blanche to be a jerk, but it is the requirement that becoming a tight-knit couple needs. Give your spouse the gift of confidence that you're going to love them enough to be honest.

2

Communication 101

As a society, we see words tossed around carelessly. Face-to-face encounters where they are spoken out loud and not typed are nearing extinction and good conversation is quickly becoming a lost art. This devolution is taking a toll on relationships. It's no wonder that so many marriages are struggling to survive, much less thrive, because of the disintegration of healthy, iron-clad communication skills.

Communication is more than mere words in a marriage. It encompasses all of the exchanges we make with our spouse. Whether it's saying, "I love you," an eye-roll, or changing out the toilet paper roll without being asked, there are messages going back and forth all the time. How we truly feel about our marriage and our spouse is found in the culmination of all of these messages.

Do we feel loved? Do we feel cherished? Do we feel valued? We answer these by how we communicate. While there are a ton of ways to communicate, we are going to focus on verbal communication for the moment.

———————————————— *Charity* ————————————————

Ted and I are firm believers in the fact that our words preserve what we want to be preserved and kill what we want killed. If I want something in Ted's life to grow, I speak to it. I tell him how much I appreciate it when he does something meaningful. If I notice his confidence is low, I speak to his strength of character and remind him of his value and successes. Because I want our love to continue to grow, I reiterate that I love him every time we talk. No, saying "I love you" every day doesn't make it lose its meaning, or make it any less special or important. It's not something to ration. Say "I love you" and say it often.

KEEP IT KIND

Communication is the life-blood of every relationship, but especially marriage. Whether it's getting on the same page or trying to keep it civil, words we speak navigate the direction of our relationship. They carry weight not only in the present but also into the future. Do you remember things your spouse or someone you cared about said to you years ago? Of course you do. That's why it is critical to become an expert at communicating with your spouse as soon as possible because your words will stay with them for years, good or bad.

How we communicate with each another has the power to shift a good marriage to great, bad to worse, and everything in between. Our dialogues set the course for the marriage because they reflect what we feel inside. They are literally the overflow of what is happening in our heart. If our heart's intention is what's best for the marriage, the words spoken will reflect that. If the heart is hurt, jealous, or even just frustrated, the words will convey that. This is why we must be mindful of what we say because the feeling behind the words can harm or bless.

One might argue that things said flippantly don't matter and that the other person should be able to get over it and not take it personally. But when we try to diminish the power of words, we are really diminishing the value of the relationship. When you said, "I do," you communicated a life-long commitment of friendship, preference, service, loyalty, respect, monogamy, support, and everything else awesome and rewarding about marriage. That promise was made with two words. Words matter.

KEEP IT KIND. NO INSULTS, SLAMS, JOKES, OR MAKING FUN AT YOUR SPOUSE'S EXPENSE.

One of the things Ted and I agreed to before we got married was we would always keep it kind. There would be no insults, slams, jokes, or making fun at each other's expense. Why? Because those things hurt and cause damage. They would replay in our minds whenever an argument came up or we were feeling slighted or offended. We place high value on each other's words because we trust they are spoken from a place of good intention, even if they don't always come out that way. Sometimes we have to take time to interpret what we said to each other or apologize for unintentionally hurting the other's feelings. But in either case, we both know and trust that what we say is not intended to harm.

When you begin to communicate intentionally, with a great marriage as your desired outcome, you evaluate a little bit longer what words should actually escape your lips. This is why you must shift the pattern of your words as soon as possible. Now you know—and knowing is half the battle. Thanks, G.I. Joe.

COMMUNICATION IS EMOTIONAL CURRENCY

Your words count for a lot to your spouse and vice versa. They are more valuable than any other person's so invest them wisely. I view Ted as my biggest and best investment. I use my words to build him up, to remind him of the greatness inside of him, and to let him know I love and desire him. I praise the things he does that mean a lot to me because I want him to keep doing them. I acknowledge and show gratitude for the ways he lightens my load.

One of the things he made me promise at the beginning of our marriage was that I wouldn't nag him, to which I replied, "Then don't make me." See what I did there? Joking aside, I didn't want to nag, so I made sure to communicate how much it meant to me when he finished each item on the seemingly never-ending honey-do list. Focusing my words on the positive outcomes caused them to grow. What is exciting now, after this much time together, is how on some things, he can predict my needs and show even more love by getting it done before I write it down.

The same thing can happen in reverse. If I decided Ted wasn't attacking the list as fast as I wanted him to and constantly brought up how long it was taking him or how dissatisfied I was, the result would be bitterness, resentment, withdrawal, and disconnection, the breeding ground for emotional distance. Also, I'm pretty sure the lag time would get longer, too, just for the irony of it.

This also applies to areas where our spouse has done something in the past that really hurt us. If the incident is continually brought up and thrown back in their face over and over again, they will feel shame. Shame is fuel for depression, addiction, and violence. When it is spelled out so plainly, it is easy to see why one would never want to send a spouse on this type of spiral, yet the repetitive shaming tactic is rampant.

There have been times in our marriage when we both needed to adjust some things about our behavior and habits. For simplicity, let's pretend Ted is the one with the issue. The process would usually begin by me bringing the issue to his attention privately during pillow talk or another quiet moment alone. Ted would acknowledge the issue that needed work and say something along the lines of "I'm going to change" or "I'm going to work on it." At the first sign that the change had not occurred, I didn't sound an alarm and jump down his throat, especially not in any kind of public setting, even in our home. You can be sure there was a look or glance that simply asked him to pause and evaluate what was happening and do his best to recoil. I have had my share of these looks from Ted as well.

> LOVE BUILDS A BRIDGE FROM WHERE WE ARE TO WHERE WE WANT TO BE AND SAYS, "I'M WITH YOU ALL THE WAY."

Later, when we go to bed, we calmly discuss what happened, affirm each other, and remind each other of the good qualities and the fact that we are still committed. These priceless discussions are money in the bank. They communicate safety, stability, unity, and love. Love covers. It doesn't seek to expose every flaw. It builds a bridge from where we are to where we want to be and says, "I'm with you all the way."

> *Now, regarding the one who started all this—the person in question who caused all this pain.... Now is the time to forgive this man and help him back on his feet. If all you do is pour on the guilt, you could very well drown him in it. My counsel now is to pour on the love.*   (2 Corinthians 2:5–8 MSG)

WHEN YOUR SPOUSE IS NOT AROUND

Something Ted and I both appreciate is that we can trust what we say about each other when we're not together. My intention is never to throw Ted under the bus or disparage his character, therefore I choose my words wisely and celebrate all of his incredible qualities. It might even be construed as bragging, but truly, I am so grateful for him and proud of him, I want people to see what I see and know more about him.

Ted is a high-caliber man. He loves me well and cherishes me. He has a servant's heart coupled with a strong desire for excellence and generosity. When word gets back to him about things I have said, of course he blushes, but then he also sits up a little taller and I can tell that his heart is smiling. It feels good to know you're appreciated and the effort you put forth is acknowledged.

I am also his defender and he is mine. If someone says something against him or his character, I do not sit idly by and say nothing. I address what was said as politely as possible, at least at first, and make sure that the person who said it knows that I will not join a smear campaign against Ted.

Now, let's be clear. I am not trying to pretend Ted doesn't have any flaws or that he is perfect every day, all day. Instead, it's a choice to intentionally talk about the best parts of him. What is so great about our relationship is that I know a lot about Ted and still think the world of him. I get to champion him and he gets to champion me. That's our role and privilege for one another. It can be yours, too.

THE BENEFIT OF THE DOUBT

It is easy to get offended or hurt when something your spouse says to you comes out wrong. Because I am a words person, I analyze and dissect things in search of all possible meanings. Okay, that may be a slight exaggeration. But in the first five to seven years of our marriage, I was actually listening for things that agreed with my own internal struggles, then getting mad at him for saying them. In reality, he didn't say or mean anything of the sort.

One of the biggest mistakes I wish I could go back and change was how I reacted to innocent comments early on in our marriage. If I got my feelings hurt, I would give him the cold shoulder and silent treatment for the whole day. While I thought I was punishing him, I was really punishing myself by not giving Ted the benefit of the doubt when something came out differently than he meant it.

Sometimes words just come out wrong. Sometimes we haven't yet shared enough of the backstory of our lives to give our spouse the sensitivity needed with certain issues. The point is, we have the choice to go full-throttle into offense mode or trust their intentions and give them a pass. You can still take time to address how the comment made you feel because, in reality, it probably had an impact and you don't have to hide that. Then give them a chance to better explain what they really meant or help them see that the subject matter, tone of voice, or gestures came across in a way that didn't feel right.

Ted

DECLARE YOUR SPOUSE'S VALUE

I love how God shows us love through His Word, not only for us as individuals, but also for marriages. The Bible is rich with declarations and promises over us. Often, these promises are woven into the many stories and parables that demonstrate how we should love each other.

Jesus said, *"The kingdom of heaven is like a merchant looking for fine pearls. When he found one of great value, he went away and sold everything he had and bought it"* (Matthew 13:45–46). If you want a successful marriage, you must apply this concept to your spouse. You must value them more than anyone else.

Charity's grandparents, Charles and Frances Hunter, definitely embodied this. They always spoke to the greatness in each other. For them, that appreciation and respect was fueled by the fact that Jesus was living inside them. This was radically expressed through how they lived their lives.

I have seen the value Charity has in my life increase throughout our marriage. She is my incredible blessing. A few years before we met, as a relatively new believer, I realized that I did not want the single life. I remember a particular sermon where the pastor was talking about answers to prayer. He said something like, "The more specific the prayer, the clearer God's answer will be." I am not sure he was even talking about finding a wife, but that was all that came to my mind.

I remember spending several nights in thought, asking myself, *What do I want in a wife?* I wanted someone who would love me as much as I loved her. I wanted someone who was great to her friends. I wanted someone who lived on her own, understood the value of a dollar and the cost of living, and had a strong work ethic. I wanted someone who was creative. Of course, I wanted someone beautiful and I even added a specific request for green eyes. Because I was so detailed, I knew I would know her when I found her.

After our third date, I could see that Charity answered all of my prayers about a wife. That is why I call her my incredible blessing. Even better, I continue to discover more wonderful attributes about Charity that I didn't even think to ask for or pray about. God in His wisdom placed these attributes inside her for me. She is wonderfully made for me and I am fashioned just right for her.

No one else has seen all of my scars, internal and external, the way Charity has over our years together. She practices increasing my value almost daily. When I told her I wanted to become a nurse, she could have said anything to give me a reason not to even try. But instead, she took my hands, looked into my eyes, and said, "I believe in you."

I didn't have the whole picture of what nursing school would take, but she knew it would be difficult and a sacrifice for our entire family. She only gave me nurturing words toward my dream. When I had any struggle, she would remind me how smart I was and how confident she was in me.

LIST THEIR GREAT ATTRIBUTES

I urge you to start looking for the great things in your spouse. When you find them and celebrate them, it causes your spouse to reflect and begin to see great things in you, too. There is nothing more valuable and empowering than when your spouse believes in, trusts, and encourages you.

Want a simple and practical way to begin? Take a moment and write down three to five things you love or admire about your spouse and share them. This exercise is beneficial even if you aren't at a good place in your marriage. One thing we know for sure is the only person we can change is ourselves. Perhaps instead of focusing energy on trying to change your spouse, you can begin by changing your behavior and your words. Ask God to help you increase your spouse's value. Even though it might be hard, it may begin the change you ultimately desire.

People around you can tell the value you place on your spouse. Friends, children, co-workers, or even bosses can attempt to jockey for position as a priority in your life. Intentionally communicate to and about your spouse in a way that makes it plain that the relationship you have with your spouse is the most important one of all.

Our children have a firm understanding that Charity and I are number one to each other. We prefer each other and our children have picked up on that. We know the message is getting through when they ask us questions like, "When I grow up, will I find someone who loves me like Mommy/Daddy loves you?"

YOUR BIGGEST INVESTMENT

Your spouse is your biggest investment on earth, the ultimate 401(k). Your communication makes deposits or withdrawals on their value, which is why this is such a key component of a strong and lasting marriage. The good news is you can begin a new investment strategy today. Maybe you've been married for a little bit and detect that the accounts are low or have breached overdraft. You have the ability to change the situation and redirect the path of your marriage.

Take time to discuss how things have been and examine what needs weren't being met. Begin to shift the culture of your home to one of honor and high value. All marriages have to navigate some tough spots. Your situation is not beyond repair. Declare the Word over your home and your relationship. Change the way you speak about your marriage to the way you want it to be.

> CHANGE THE WAY YOU SPEAK ABOUT YOUR MARRIAGE TO THE WAY YOU WANT IT TO BE.

We love to grow vegetables, herbs, and fruit. The plants first show up as balled-up buds. Then comes a blossom, from which the fruit or vegetable begins to appear. We must plant, water, fertilize, tend, and wait before we can harvest the crops.

Progress, too, takes time to bud and blossom. Don't go looking for fully-ripened change in your spouse immediately. You will be disappointed and they will feel discouraged. Search for the buds, the small shifts of new beginnings, and encourage them as they bloom and produce.

3

Ask for What You Need

Communication is a big, broad word and rather than give you our thoughts and some vague directions for male/female communications or how to communicate effectively, we thought, "What if we talk about *WHAT* to communicate instead?" We are the kind of people who learn well with specific directions and examples. We hope you do, too.

These are some of the conversations that have helped our marriage immensely because they carry the true emotions we often hide and disguise behind the smoke and mirrors of our actions. Again, you may not find yourself in these same situations, but you may be able to use them to apply to your marriage.

Charity

WHAT? CAN'T YOU READ MY MIND?

Romance novels, movies, TV shows, and magazines love to paint unrealistic pictures of what modern loving relationships look like. I have a strong disdain for "princess movies" that make girls think that a handsome prince will rescue them and solve all of their problems. Contrary to popular belief, men *cannot* read minds. This was something that only took me a few years to come to terms with regarding Ted. For a while, I believed in and hoped for the best when it came to his emotional intelligence toward me. I just knew that with enough training, he could reach relational perfection.

Alas, I'm not a magician and I could not change his DNA. He was never going to be able to sense my every want or desire. I began to realize that if I wanted something from him, I was going to have to ask for it. How embarrassing, right? That's what I thought in the beginning. But again, the choice was to suffer in silence or get what I needed. There is a big gap between the pain of not getting what you want and the joy of actually getting it. However, that gap instantly closed each time I gave Ted the information he really wanted so he could meet my needs.

CLEAN OR CLUTTER?

While sharing similar core values, Ted and I are remarkably different. One of the areas we were nearly polar opposites at the beginning was in the area of cleanliness. I was your typical neat freak, type A, everything has its place kind of person. Ted's standard was, "As long as there aren't any bugs, we're fine." Okay, that might be a slight exaggeration, but the truth is he wasn't bothered by clutter, dust, clothes on the floor, or the lack of vacuum lines.

My initial interpretation of his neglect was that he didn't care about me or how a messy one-bedroom apartment made me feel. We were crowded in that tight space, especially with my grand piano taking over what should have been the dining room. I saw every little thing and was offended that he did not.

Our one tiny bathroom had white linoleum tile. Why anyone would have solid white tile is beyond me. Every time I went into the bathroom, I saw all of the hair and dust that had accumulated on the floor. Out of pure curiosity and experimentation, I would wait to see how long it would take for Ted to notice the filth. It was agony.

Is he ever going to do anything about this stuff? Did I marry a slob? Does he expect me to fall into the gender role of housekeeper? If so, he has another think coming! No way am I the domestic goddess! We are equal partners, so we both clean!

After about the fourth day of my solo, silent "standoff," I realized Ted had no idea there even was a standoff. He did not know I was running an experiment measuring how long it would take him to notice the dust and strands of hair. He didn't even know it bothered me. When I mentioned it, he said, "What dust?" I'm pretty sure steam was shooting out from my ears by this point.

"Do you not see it every time you go to the bathroom?!"

I think I was actually grossed out that he didn't notice it. What kind of cleanliness standards did he have?

To his surprise, I began unloading on him, with shock and awe, how his lack of cleanliness made me feel. He looked like a deer in the headlights. He truly had no idea what I was talking about and never had any intention of making me feel that he didn't care.

ASK AND YE SHALL RECEIVE

Once I calmed down, he gently said, "If you want me to clean the bathroom floor, just ask me."

Could it be that simple? I wanted him to read my mind. I didn't really want to say anything out loud. But here, he gave me the opportunity to simply ask and it would get done. *How profound!*

Now, after years of marriage and four children, I am fully capable of stepping over piles of stuff to get to my office and get working. I don't know if I'm a rehabilitated clean freak or just an inoculated mom-preneur trying to survive. Either way, I have chilled out and Ted has stepped up his game.

This balance is one of the coolest things about marriage. Areas where we started out as opposites are now finding their way to a middle ground. Each day, we get into a better rhythm, making life really enjoyable. This is in no way a claim that we have reached perfection, but improvement is improvement.

Ted

TOUCH ME, BABY

I know that everyone who meets Charity thinks she is amazing, which she is, but one of the things that I needed from her early on in our marriage was more touching. Touch is my main love language. It gives me a strong sense of connection to Charity, so the more, the better. Of course, sexual touch is great, but even her rubbing my back or running her fingers through my hair was something I really wanted when we were relaxing together.

During the day, she would always rub my back, hold my hand, or pull me close, but at night, it felt like she was sort of avoiding me. We would do our nighttime rituals of teeth-brushing and face-washing, maybe have a "married tickle fight," and, of course, Charity's favorite thing: pillow talk. But when it was time to wind down, all I wanted was for her to be close and touch me.

I thought that if I rubbed her back and shoulders while she was lying there beside me, it would give her the idea this was something

I wanted quid pro quo. But once I turned over with my back to her, she stayed put and fell blissfully asleep. I was giving her what I wanted, expecting her to reciprocate in the same fashion intuitively. My unspoken expectation was going unmet. With my guy friends, if someone helps me with a project, it makes me want to help them with a project; if they pick up the check at one our hang times, it makes me want to pick up the check at the next.

I thought Charity knew the code: "What I do for you, I would like done for me in return." Nope. She did not. Not her fault. It took some time before I told her how I felt. At first, I thought she was just tired. We were both working several jobs then, so by the time we fell into bed, we were exhausted. I knew it wasn't an attraction issue because she was all over me the rest of the time and very engaged.

Charity is constantly thinking and processing the day's events, tomorrow's activities, plans for the future, and anything else that could possibly concern her or our family, so sleep sometimes evades her. When I would rub her back, her thoughts would settle and focus on what I was doing rather than all the details that didn't deserve her attention at that hour. And she fell asleep much faster. I had created a pattern for her. It was like I was her melatonin, so soothing and necessary. But I wanted that, too!

Fortunately, I have no trouble falling asleep most nights, so I would chalk it up to, "She needs this more than me." That worked for a little while. There I was, so open and honest in every other area, but I realized I wasn't being open with her about this desire.

One night, when my need for touch went from desire to full-on got-to-have-it, I spoke up and said, "Will you rub my back after I rub yours?" To my surprise, it worked. She rubbed my back. She asked me if this was something I wanted more often. "Ummm, yes please."

She told me she honestly hadn't thought about rubbing my back in bed before. She wasn't withholding something she knew I needed; she simply didn't know I needed it. Needless to say, many back rubs later, I'm glad I communicated what I needed to her so I could reap the benefits of us having an even deeper connection emotionally and physically.

Charity

WRITTEN NOTES

Ted has always been very gifted in the area of writing from the heart, which is perfect for a person like me who loves words. I think my love of receiving notes started with my mom. When I went away to college, she literally wrote me a card or a note three or four times a week. At the beginning of the semester, I would tape the cards to my dorm room door; it quickly filled up from top to bottom. This is one of the predominant ways my mom showed me she loves me, so after a while, it became a way that I wanted to receive love.

I told Ted from the very beginning that I like getting written letters and notes because these not only communicated love, but also enabled me to go back and read them at any time and remember all of that love. I have boxes and boxes of meaningful letters and notes that I've kept throughout the years. Whenever I am in a sentimental mood, I can go back and read letters from my grandparents, mom, friends, mentors, and especially Ted. It is like a heart-love explosion when I go back through them. Needless to say, I appreciate it when Ted writes me letters.

Notes are nowhere on Ted's radar as far as love languages go. He doesn't think about them on a regular basis, so he only writes them sporadically. I could let time go by and bitterness increase if it has been a while since the last note, or I could simply ask him to write me one. Yes, he feels bad when I have to remind him, but he appreciates that I tell him what I need, giving him the chance to do it for me. This type of honesty and fulfillment of needs halts the growth and spread of resentment, which is the root of many marital problems.

BEYOND PILLOW TALK

The bedroom is a key place for both husband and wife to ask for what they need. As a modern woman and wife, I express myself and have an opinion about what goes on. In fact, I enjoy taking the lead just as much as being led.

Sexual personality types know no gender. While men often get labeled as the ones looking for excitement and variety in the bedroom, it can sometimes be a woman's need, too. After going through our childbearing years of sex having to be very gentle, careful, or put on hold, Ted had to mentally get back to how things were before.

I was struggling in this season because I wanted the passion back, some surprises, and some things shaken up every now and then. On top of the difficult years we had, Ted's personality is consistently consistent. His modus operandi is, "If it ain't broke, don't fix it." Yes, what he was doing was "working," but I wanted more than the reliable, tried-and-true approach.

As someone who creates incredibly high expectations, I set myself up for disappointment after disappointment, hoping Ted would flip the passion switch on his own. I wanted him to reclaim his boldness. To be honest, I was scared of getting bored and having a wandering heart.

The first conversation we had went awkwardly well. All seemed to be cleared up until it came time to try it out. *Whoa, too much hair pulling! I didn't mean you had to turn into a caveman,* I thought to myself as I rolled over, frustrated and disappointed. I thought we were clear? Yet, in his defense, he tried.

I wasn't going to give up. And friends, you shouldn't either. Things worth having are worth doing the work it takes to get them. I knew I needed to express my desires in a different way. I continued to do my best to communicate that it wasn't really aggression that I craved. I wanted him to come at me testosterone blazing, confident and hungry.

COMMIT IN YOUR HEART TO NOT GIVE UP EVEN WHEN ASKING THE FIRST TIME DIDN'T WORK.

So a few weeks later, I circled back to ask. This time, he wanted more specifics—almost a checklist, which did seem to take some of the fun out of it initially. However, over time, and with open lines of communication, we were able to find what worked for both of us.

THIS is the stuff that builds your marital confidence. Being able to work through things and come out on the other side is like a notch in the belt. Determine to keep trying and ask God for help in how to say it. Commit in your heart to not give up even when asking the first time didn't work.

HIS NEEDS

Ted's needs are pretty streamlined. He needs to feel loved, appreciated, desired, and fulfilled. I do my best to anticipate his needs and provide for them before he has to ask, but there are occasional times when either I've been working too hard or have been distracted and dropped the ball.

Thankfully, he doesn't wait around for me to guess what he wants. He just says it or gives me "the look." I appreciate his gentle yet direct approach because for me, feeling like I missed one of his needs sometimes made me feel like a bad wife. The pursuit of being a perfect wife is something I still struggle with, but he encourages me daily that I am exactly what he wants.

It was hard sometimes because I would try to defend or justify why I wasn't meeting that need, when in reality he wasn't mad, he was simply communicating. He was aware of most if not all of the circumstances; he was just giving me the opportunity to give attention where he needed it.

When your husband or wife comes to you asking for something, don't immediately jump on the defensive. It probably took some courage on their part to even say anything, so give them the consideration of reflecting and figuring out a way to add what they are asking for into your plans.

A BIG NO-NO

One thing that drives me crazy—and I know I'm not alone in this—is passive aggression. This back-handed, annoying style of trying to get what you want has no place in marriage, or any relationship really. If this is how you are used to getting what you want, grow up and stop it.

Don't say one thing yet mean another. If you want your husband or wife to believe you when you say something, then only speak the truth. You are hurting yourself and the trust level of your relationship when you beat around the bush.

You may have seen this in your parents' home when you were growing up. Your dad may have told your mom, "That pie was almost as good as my mother's." She may have told him, "Well, I guess that raise is all you can expect since you didn't go to college." If your spouse asks if you're okay with him going out with friends and you say "sure" while putting on a cold shoulder/sad puppy act because you really want him to stay but you don't want to say no, you're being passive-aggressive.

> WHEN YOU ARE TRUTHFUL AND NOT CONTROLLING OR MANIPULATIVE, YOUR SPOUSE CAN TRUST THAT IF YOU SAY YOU NEED THEM, THEY SHOULD BE THERE FOR YOU.

Sadly, women are guilty of this type of manipulative behavior quite often. You might actually be feeling conflicted inside because you want them to have time with their friends *and* be with you. If that's the case, say it! At least be honest about your feelings. If you are in a place where you truly need time with your spouse, make that clear. When you have a history of being truthful and not controlling or manipulative, your spouse can trust that if you say you need them, they should be there for you without question.

HONORING THE REQUEST

The other half of asking for what we need is the response we get to give when our spouse asks *us* for something.

When I was a child, there were times my dad thought I was lying to him when I wasn't. I would say I was not feeling well or had a terrible headache and he would say, "Of course, you don't feel well. It's Thursday." For a long time, this conditioned me to stifle and minimize my needs as they were probably petty, not worthy of attention, or maybe not even real.

I remember how hard it was to tell Ted I had a headache early on in our marriage. I was literally terrified he wouldn't believe me. I needed to be in a quiet, dark room...but I wanted him with me. I personally don't like to be alone when I don't feel well. I wanted to feel his comfort and support, but didn't want to sound selfish or lazy. We were both working so hard at that time that lying around was a luxury.

I cried as Ted crawled into bed with me because it conveyed so much love and trust. I'm sure he had plenty to do but he decided what I needed took priority in that moment. Once the medicine kicked in, I was able to sleep for a bit. I woke up not only feeling better but also feeling worth more.

THE GIFT OF BELIEF

Giving your spouse the gift of belief in their needs goes a long way. So many of us grew up with needs unmet because we were raised by imperfect people. It was our sincere goal and intention to raise our kids in such a way that they wouldn't need therapy. After the first one, we thought, "Okay, maybe a little therapy." By the time we had four, we were asking ourselves if we should set up a fund for therapy because we realized we were never going to be able to meet *all* of their needs despite our best efforts.

We intentionally didn't include advice on parenting in this book because so much of good parenting is good "spousing." When we keep each other's love-tank full, we are better at everything— better parents, better friends, better employees, better neighbors, all because we are not in starvation mode.

As parents, we present a unified front. We don't look for love from our children to replace our spousal love. We aren't insecure, so we don't try to be our children's favorite. Our marital goals are up to date and remind us that our kids are only with us for a little bit while our marriage is forever. Keeping this in mind helps us to parent as a true team. Like any good team, we do our best to relieve each other's burdens. We can both sense when the other has had a rough day and then take up the slack where the kids, mealtimes, chores, or other duties come into play. The longer you're married, the better you become at anticipating your spouse's needs.

WHERE DO THESE NEEDS COME FROM?

While it may not be obvious right off the bat, many needs we have reach way back into our childhood. Maybe there was food scarcity, fighting, abandonment, lack of engagement, infidelity, insignificance, abuse, or other issues. Much of what we are able to do is meet our spouses where they are at and help to mend the gaps in their hearts.

While neither of us are psychologists, we both have spent a great deal of our lives caring for and listening to people. If we were to boil it down, we all need to feel important, special, noticed, cared for, and needed. We also need to feel that those we love are loyal to us.

If your spouse is asking for something that isn't on your personal preference list, take time to reflect on what the deeper need is. This will help you have compassion and grace even if you don't resonate with the specific need itself. Listening is key to understanding and gaining insight. As you peel the layers back, story by story, often what is found are pockets where the love they wanted to feel is missing and the attention they so deeply craved is absent. With every faithful act of love and loyalty, we begin to fill those empty spots and help them feel whole and wholly loved.

4

Conflict Resolution

Marriage does put you in some precarious situations. Just like the first few steps on the ropes course we mentioned in our preface, the first years of marriage are all about establishing communication, rhythm, trust, and finding a balance.

Each decision that puts the marriage first, each opportunity to resolve a conflict, each tragedy you have worked through together, and each success you've handled well strengthens your belief system in one another. It reinforces that your spouse will be there when you need them and you will be there when they need you.

Charity

MOMENTS THAT MATTER

One of my Launch Author Coaching clients wrote a book about life being like a strand of pearls and how we should collect the moments (or pearls) that matter— those defining moments of love. When I reflect on our marriage, the moments that matter most are the ones when what could have broken us actually brought us closer.

> THE MOMENTS THAT COULD HAVE BROKEN US ACTUALLY BROUGHT US CLOSER.

It is hard to know the depths of love until it is tested or experienced. On May 4, 2002, Ted and I publicly declared our love for each other by getting married. At the time, it seemed like we loved each other to the max, like there was no room for our love to get any bigger. Our friends called us "sickening love puppies" and we lived up to that name. But that love hadn't been tested or proven. It is amazing to see what depth love can reach when it is a choice even amid challenges and conflict.

Ted

Conflict is a hot topic. I like to say that it's one of my favorites because we approach it openly and honestly. We don't fear having conflict. We embrace what it reveals and look forward to the amazing growth that comes from resolving issues and difficulties we face together.

Any time two people share space, responsibilities, money, bathrooms, and children, conflict can and frankly should happen. If there is no conflict to resolve, then how are you growing as a couple? I'm not suggesting there should be constant conflict, but different stages in your relationship will have moments of decision, choices of which paths to take, struggles, exhaustion, and variables to navigate that need full input from both of you.

As we shared in chapter one, Charity and I do not see or respond to issues and difficulties the same way. Often, we both initially believe we have a clear direction or response to an issue. Out of honor and respect for each other's opinion, we discuss it and decide together what course we will take. We always move forward united.

I freely admit that frequently, Charity has the more logical, thought-out approach because her mind can see twelve steps down the road. I, on the other hand, either take forever to deliberate or jump with blind trust or gut feelings. We need each other's strengths and styles and it's exciting to see how each issue draws out a great combination from both of us.

IF YOU CAN, AVOID IT

While conflict and its resolution are powerful growth tools, we aren't suggesting you seek to engage in them as much as possible. In fact, we suggest you avoid *creating* conflict. This isn't the same as avoiding conflict. You can often avoid creating conflict through discovery. That's a legal term I picked up from watching *Law and Order*. I can best describe the action of discovery as playing, "What would (your spouse's name) do?" and see how your partner would handle different scenarios.

For example, I remember asking Charity if she would rather buy a car or continue to lease one. She told me her father said something along the lines of, "You will always have a car payment, so just lease something you like." She also said she thought that was horrible advice and she didn't plan to lease a car again. I was glad to hear her thoughts because at the time, she was riding out the tail end of a lease. I saw the potential for conflict coming if she thought leasing vehicles was a good idea. Discovering it wasn't before the time was up definitely eliminated the concern I had and allowed me to move on.

> STUDY YOUR SPOUSE.
> WHEN IN CONFLICT,
> LEARN WHAT APPROACHES
> PRODUCE THE BEST OUTCOMES.

The beauty of loving for a lifetime is you have the opportunity to discover a lot about your spouse. Fanning your flame of curiosity about them drives connection, especially in the area of conflict and its resolution. Study your spouse. When in conflict, learn what approaches produce the best outcomes.

If your spouse doesn't like to talk in the heat of the moment, give them time and space. If your spouse can't stand the thought of the two of you being in disagreement, give them the gift of opening up and discussing the situation.

Don't waste time splitting hairs over petty stuff. If you notice that what you are fighting about is something that doesn't really matter, relent. Admit the disagreement is frivolous, kiss, and make up. I'm not saying you should shuffle fundamental issues under the rug, but I am suggesting you have the power to evaluate and end a silly argument.

IN PEACE TIME

Discovery can also happen in times of peace. When you're together, you can show your desire to know your spouse by asking questions about their vision for the future, preferences, experiences, and overall feelings. Being pursued is one of the highest compliments you can show your spouse, so pursue their feelings and locate their heart on major matters. Some sample discovery questions are:

+ How do you feel about the way we discipline our children?

+ What is something I do that makes you happy?

+ What are your least favorite household chores?

+ How do you feel about where we live in relationship to our families?

+ What is something I could make easier for you?

+ How should the toilet paper roll go, over or under? (Okay, maybe that's not a major issue for you, but some people actually fight over this.)

+ What do I do that expresses love to you?

+ Is there anything you want to be doing in the next five years that you're not doing now?

+ What is something you would like to change?

As you learn the inspiring answers to these and other questions, you will receive clues about what makes your spouse tick. Remember these when conflict arises to repair the communication bridge and restore intimacy. Remind your spouse how valuable they are to you and own any part of the problem that's yours. Marriage can be a powerful union when you both lean into each other during challenges or conflicts.

MARRIAGE CAN BE A POWERFUL UNION WHEN YOU BOTH LEAN INTO EACH OTHER DURING CHALLENGES OR CONFLICTS.

Work to find common ground and strengthen your bond to each other. Some issues require more than a one-time discussion so be willing to stay at the table and, if needed, take the issue to a neutral party to see if what you are saying matches what you mean.

Not all issues will resolve in your favor or your spouse's. In these cases, priority must be given to finding an agreement together to resolve any conflict impasse.

In high school, I loved riding my motorcycle. I was single and had no responsibilities. Motorcycles cost less to maintain than a car, they get amazing gas mileage, and—big plus—they're a blast to ride. Before we had children, I thought about getting another motorcycle instead of driving my gas-guzzling truck. Gas prices were high, so I thought Charity would totally support my brilliant, money-saving idea.

I quickly found out she is vehemently opposed to motorcycles. I asked her about it and got an earful. She was, and will always be, concerned for my safety. To her, the thought of me riding a motorcycle was like playing Russian roulette with only one empty chamber. So we agreed that a motorcycle would not be a mode of transportation for my entire life.

You might be thinking, *Awww, she made you give up something that you liked?* But I decided that the stress it would put on her was not worth the feeling of wind blowing through my not-so-thick hair.

We had a conflict about another subject, too: tattoos. I'm opposed to them. Charity already had two and I didn't want her to get any more. So we compromised. I said, "You don't get any more tattoos and I won't get a motorcycle."

I am not sure I can make a case against tattoos that can compare with the anti-motorcycle case Charity can rattle off at a moment's notice, but I'll give it a go. First, tattoos are rarely done well. After a year or two or five, even the best tattoo looks like faded magic marker. Second, tattoos are addictive for most people. It's rare to see someone with only one. Just think about anyone you know who has a tattoo and ask yourself, "Did they stop with one?" No. Ninety percent have more than one and the other 10 percent just have not found the right tribal, barbed wire, or ivy pattern that speaks to them. (No, these aren't real statistics, just my impression.) Third, tattoos are permanent. Okay, there are removal methods, but they come with their own issues.

Charity

One of the joys of writing this book together has been discovering that the feelings we have about these issues are still so strong. Countless threats of motorcycle purchases and additional tattoos have been made over the years, mostly in joking. We both respect how much these things mean to each other and we just stay way back from the line.

A MASTER OF TRIVIAL FRUSTRATION

Trivial fights and frustrations can strip away the joy of married life if not seen for what they are: trivial. Whether it's the growing pile of clothes on the floor, the used sweetener packets left out on the kitchen counter every day, or the battle over toilet seat position, in the long run, these things don't matter.

I remember reading a blog about a woman who had recently lost her husband. They were both young and his death came out of nowhere. She expressed regret over how she made a big deal over the underwear on the floor and the bed not being made and how she wished she had focused on what really mattered and enjoyed him more.

Hopefully, most of us will not have to learn this lesson. If we are wise, we will learn from the mistakes and missteps of others willing to share their stories and correct our own behavior so that we don't end up with deep regret.

I used to be a master of trivial frustration. Because I was such a mess on the inside, keeping a very clean house was my way of controlling at least one environment. Besides the dusty, white bathroom floor, our one-bedroom apartment came equipped with the smallest kitchen ever. It was just six-by-eight feet with four short-style cabinets and no pantry. This tight space required immense organization to function at all, so we had our dishes in one cabinet and pots and pans in two more, leaving just one cabinet for food stuff.

VINEGAR IS *NOT* A SAUCE!

This food cabinet had separate sections for spices, sauces, condiments, and canned goods or packaged foods. All was working perfectly until one day when we came home from the store with red wine vinegar. Ted began putting the groceries away as I closed the door and brought over the last of the bags. Right then, I saw it. Ted put the vinegar with the sauces.

"That's not a sauce!"

To Ted, it was liquid, therefore it was a sauce. In my mind, it was a condiment, *way* different from a sauce, and it belonged in the condiment section.

We spent the next ten or twenty minutes debating who was right and where this bottle of vinegar should go, because for Pete's sake, we would need to be able to find it when we went looking for it in our one and only tiny food cabinet. For some reason, it seemed important in that fleeting moment. I think what was really going on was that we were both frustrated with how small our apartment was and this vinegar was just a reminder of that. We made it the scapegoat for our underlying issue.

Now we look back on this event and laugh because we know how immature we both were back then, especially me. We both should have acquiesced and let the vinegar go wherever it could fit.

A MEANINGLESS TROPHY

Trivial issues drive tiny wedges into the fine cracks of relationships. It's essential to recognize when it simply doesn't matter. It's not worth the energy, the dissonance, or even winning. Because at the end of the day, all you can say is you won a silly little argument. Yeah, congratulations. Here's your trophy. Meanwhile, your relationship is now strained.

This stuff is just plain old bickering. You know, the kind of thing you yell at your kids for doing because it's annoying and tiring. Over time, bickering wears you down. It's like a Trojan horse that snuck in a bunch of bitterness and ran off with the fun.

> TRIVIAL ISSUES DRIVE TINY WEDGES INTO THE FINE CRACKS OF RELATIONSHIPS. IT'S ESSENTIAL TO RECOGNIZE WHEN IT SIMPLY DOESN'T MATTER.

TO VENT OR ZIP IT

One issue that thrives in the right environment is venting. With just the right amount of hunger, tiredness, disappointment, embarrassment, or frustration, the desire to vent your feelings is almost insatiable. We play out a few sassy exchanges in our mind, feel the quick little rush of the imaginary scenario, and suddenly want more. We want so badly to hear the words, "You were right" as we are now inconvenienced by our partner's slip-up.

Venting immediately changes the climate from honor, respect, and intimacy to shame, blame, and distance. It is the opposite of what love is designed to do, which is to cover or absorb a litany of mistakes. It is like coating your spouse with verbal slime; it's hard for them to wash it off.

A simple yet not always easy shift in those instances where it would "feel better" in the moment to unleash is to offer grace in the place of frustration. Offer support instead of abandoning them to clean the mess up themselves. Believe me, your time will come and what type of response would you want? This is extremely relevant if you have kids around watching you. They are waiting to see if you are going to disavow each other or remain a team. They keep track of how you respond in those situations. Following our example, they learn how they should treat their friends, siblings, and others. As painful as it is sometimes to swallow our need to be *right*, it goes down much better than the aftertaste of airing it all out.

THROUGH THEIR LENS

Throughout this book, we encourage you to identify, study, and understand your spouse in a fresh way. Our culture portrays wives as if they are always looking at husbands as projects that need to be fixed or creatures that need to be trained, and husbands like they are aloof, stupid, or too confused by women to understand their needs. For the good of our marriages, we need to rise above these stereotypes.

It will no doubt take effort to understand your spouse. It is easy to be confused by each other's behaviors because so much of who we are stems from impressions or experiences in our childhood that may have resulted in insecurities or unspoken fears.

Ted

DON'T ALL WOMEN WANT DIAMONDS?

One example of this type of behavior confusion happened a few years into our marriage. We had paid off all of our debt and life was great. Since I love to spoil Charity, one day, I decided I wanted to get her some nice diamond earrings. My motivation was to bring her joy and excitement. When I shared my plans with her, however, she began to cry in distress. Yes, that's right. She was frustrated and crying because I wanted to buy her diamond earrings.

What kind of woman doesn't want diamonds? I was so confused. I could have been angry that she wasn't grateful and didn't appreciate my thoughtfulness, or at least offended by her underwhelming response, but I knew something else was going on. I just didn't quite know what it was. What's crazy was that she couldn't articulate it either. When I asked her why she was upset, she said it wasn't because she didn't feel worthy of nice things or that she didn't like diamond earrings, but…. She couldn't say what was wrong.

> LOOK FOR WAYS TO UNDERSTAND YOUR SPOUSE'S BEHAVIOR BEFORE COMBATING IT.

We need to look for ways to understand our spouse's behavior before combating it. I remember praying and asking God to reveal the source of Charity's reaction. The next day, while working overtime, my prayer was answered.

You see, for a few years, we both worked extra jobs to get out of the debt I brought with me into our marriage. We sacrificed many things to get to a stable financial position. From my perspective, we had done the hard work and it was time to enjoy the fruit of our labors. Taking care of and spoiling Charity brings me joy. Giving her something of value, like diamond earrings, was one way I could express my love for her.

Charity's perspective was far different. She had no idea that I really needed to have the freedom to spoil her. Her subconscious issue was what the earrings represented: less time with me. At that point in our marriage, the earrings would have cost more than two weeks' pay. Charity would rather spend more time with me than get diamond earrings. So it wasn't the gift, but what the gift would ultimately cost her that made her cry in frustration.

While I was working overtime, my thought was that the extra money would be enough to get a nice gift for her. She viewed my working overtime as losing quality time with me. A true blessing for her was the relief she experienced when I told her what God revealed to me about her underlying issue. I was able to give words to the deep feelings she had, but couldn't express. This revelation alone made her so happy that earrings would have paled in comparison.

Once we saw things from each other's perspective, we could both express our positions in a healthy way and grow closer. Now we are able to balance my need to give her gifts with her need to have quality time. She is able to accept tokens of my affection and I am excited for every moment we get to spend together. The Bible reminds us, *"It is more blessed to give than to receive"* (Acts 20:35). We know this is true. But if we do not learn how to *receive* love from our spouse, we rob them of that joy.

NEVER GO TO SLEEP ANGRY

One of the biggest tenets of our marriage code is to never go to sleep angry. Thankfully, we don't fight or argue a lot, but on those rare and challenging occasions when we do, avoiding each other feels like the easiest thing to do in the moment.

When we got married, we promised we would resolve whatever the day's issues were that day rather than stringing them on to another day. Most of these types of arguments stemmed from frustrations or comments that nudged our no-insult rule, while others were usually unintentional hurt feelings. Because Ted's words mean so much to me, I take what he says very seriously. I believe he is always telling me the truth, so if something comes out sideways or hurtful, I take it personally.

The usual pattern was offense, silence, and distance, with hours of inner turmoil for both of us. Night would come and all I could think about was that we were going to have to talk about the "big event" before we fell asleep. We would brush our teeth a mere sink apart and act like the other person wasn't there. No eye contact, no talking, just ritual.

Because the rule stated that we would not go to sleep angry, the stalemate would sometimes last until 2 or 3 a.m. We would lie in bed, both of us on the furthest edge of our side, backs to each other, wide awake, stubbornly remaining silent. For me, my brain was playing out every possible scenario of how this was going to go.

Will he just start this already? I wanted Ted to apologize first because, after all, he hurt my feelings. On the other hand, *he* thought I made a big deal out of nothing and I should apologize. Or he thought he did nothing wrong so an apology wasn't necessary. And so on.

It took us a few long years to realize that we were both wasting precious time—time we would never get back. I distinctly remember an incident in which Ted and I were in the "pay off debt phase" of our marriage, each working two or three jobs. It was a Saturday morning and we had the whole day to spend together until our restaurant night shifts began. I was so excited to spend the day with him. We had plans to be-bop all around Nashville to run errands, with lots of hand-holding, kissing, and conversation thrown in.

Neither of us remember exactly what was said, but Ted made a comment that struck a chord in me…and I just shut down. We still had all of those errands to run, but after that comment, there was no hand-holding, kissing, or conversation. We just drove around, both facing forward to avoid eye contact. What was supposed to be an afternoon of deepening our connection and growing our love ended up being a total loss.

Later that night, after both of our shifts, we came home physically and emotionally exhausted. The hurt from the comment turned into embarrassment and regret. I should have handled it immediately so we could move on with our day together. I became angry with myself; instead of letting Ted know he hurt my feelings—which I made quite obvious, but without the invitation to reconcile and make things right—I wasted our whole day. I robbed myself of the very thing I wanted most: closeness and connection.

My pride, fear, insecurity, and stubbornness won that day. We will never get that time back, despite the number of times I wish I could have a do-over. Friends, this is truly one of the lessons I wish someone would have shared with me sooner. I would much rather learn from someone else's mistakes than pay the price to learn like this. God knows how much time I wasted being upset over things that did not matter in the long run.

I want you to hear me on this: If your feelings are hurt by something your spouse likely didn't even mean, take a moment and think about the grand scheme of things. Diffuse the urge to be offended. In the words of Cher, "If it doesn't matter in five years, it doesn't matter."

THE "NO COUCH" RULE

In addition to the "no going to sleep angry" agreement, we also agreed to a "no couch" rule. We did not get married to argue. We did not get married to be apart. We wanted there to be no room for division in our marriage and that meant not giving any space to hurt, anger, bitterness, or resentment to set up camp and grow.

For over half of our married life, we have had roommates and or family members living with us. Nothing helps to hold you to your word like other people watching. Having that kind of accountability was probably a blessing in disguise. We didn't see it as such at the time, but looking back, we appreciate how it helped us uphold this standard.

ARMED AND DANGEROUS

When you love someone deeply and feel that love in return, it frees you to be extraordinarily vulnerable. You share the deep, dark secrets, the areas of weakness and shame, moments of utter humiliation, and everything else on the "Do Not Speak Of" list. In this vulnerable state, you also open up about things that tick you off, drive you crazy, or annoy you, unknowingly arming your spouse with the combination to your nuclear detonation.

The knowledge of these hot buttons is ideally shared in hopes that your spouse will avoid pressing them at all costs. However, when there is conflict, they can become a playground. If you are a newlywed, you are probably thinking, "No way would I ever do that." To you, we say, "Here's hoping." For real, here's hoping. It's like someone telling you not to do something and then, when you want to get back at them for some offense, that's all you can think about doing. Not a big deal in times of peace, but if the def-con level ever changed, it's the first thing on your list of planned attacks.

Now, we all would like our marriages to resemble fields of flowers and we can strive toward that. But when a fire breaks out and threatens that field, when something breaks in the relationship, our loyalty to our spouse is tested.

Trust is forged during the difficult times. It is tested by fire. Your spouse is watching and waiting to see what you will do with the knowledge you have about their insecurities, weaknesses, points of shame, and other issues when you are in a place of contention. Be very careful to not break that trust, even when you are at odds. If it is damaged or broken in the process, it's hard to get it back.

When you disagree, keep the fight clean. Stay on-topic and deal with one issue at a time. Don't pull the trigger on peripheral areas that make your spouse hurt deeply simply to appease your ego. There will be far more jewels in your crown from leaving these types of things unsaid.

WHO IS THE BRAVEST?

> The first to apologize is the bravest. The first to forgive is the strongest. The first to forget is the happiest.
>
> —Zig Ziglar

This quote sums it up beautifully. It's something I try to remember every day. I am pretty sure that out of the two of us, Ted is the "happiest," but we take turns being brave and strong.

Apologizing when you know you were in the wrong is brave. Apologizing when you didn't mean to do something wrong it is even braver. But perhaps the bravest move of all is apologizing even when it wasn't your fault. There have been times when both Ted and I have apologized simply to get us back on the same page and reopen the lines of communication. Apologizing is an act of humility and deference that helps to bring down your spouse's defensive walls.

IT TAKES TEAMWORK

In a marriage, you're on the same team. One of you doesn't "win" an argument while the other "loses." You win together or you lose together. Period. If either of you chooses to be "right," neither of you will be happy.

Most arguments, while they may seem unique, stem from the simple yet vital need to feel secure. Fighting shakes and tests the marital foundation. Committing acts of service, showing preference for your spouse, and reinforcing their value to you, even on a day when they don't seem to deserve it, reinforces it. It takes bravery to speak to the good in your spouse, especially when you're not seeing it. Don't start a fight just to see how well your marriage is built.

> APOLOGIZING IS AN ACT OF HUMILITY AND DEFERENCE THAT HELPS TO BRING DOWN YOUR SPOUSE'S DEFENSIVE WALLS.

WHO IS THE STRONGEST?

Offering forgiveness to a sincere apology does take strength and not just in that moment or on that day. Telling your spouse you forgive them and meaning it says more than just, "Thank you for admitting you were wrong." It says, "I will no longer bring up this offense or hold it against you." It truly is the exercise and practice of extending grace. Grace is a muscle that few choose to develop, much to their own detriment. It carries, covers, rescues, and preserves the heart of the person to whom it is extended. One of the most challenging things about love is that it must not keep a record of wrongs. (See 1 Corinthians 13:5.)

Offering your spouse forgiveness doesn't mean that you get to bank things to hold against them in the future. Constantly reminding them of things they did wrong causes them to feel shame. It creates a mindset that, "I can never exceed the level of my failures, so why try?"

Forgiveness in love is continually believing the best in them, believing the offense was a lapse in judgment, rather than a character flaw.

ONE OF THE MOST CHALLENGING THINGS ABOUT LOVE IS THAT IT MUST NOT KEEP A RECORD OF WRONGS.

Caveat: We are in no way suggesting that you should remain in an abusive relationship. The offenses and hurts we are talking about are the ones that are inadvertent or rare. If you are in a relationship with someone who verbally, mentally, or physically abuses you, please seek professional help.

Charity

WHO IS THE HAPPIEST?

For us, Ted is by far the happiest because I have to remind myself to forget. I can't be the only one, right?! Ted has the ability to easily forget the things I have done that hurt him. It is either a gift or a Jedi skill. I am still trying to figure out which one and then how to master it.

There is something very brave about apologizing first, especially in cases where you were not the initiator. When you set aside your "rightness" for the sake of peace, you are blessed. We try to remember that peace is one of our ultimate goals in our home, not "right" or "wrong." That peace grows best when there are no ill feelings between us. If you didn't happen to be the one who asked for forgiveness, then be sure to be the one who offers it when asked.

You never know when you will be the one who needs a good dose of forgiveness. If you stay married any length of time, there is a good chance that you will do or say something that causes damage, so sow seeds of forgiveness, gentleness, and humility in the reconciliation process.

A happy marriage is the union of two good forgivers.
—Ruth Bell Graham

PURSUE PEACE

Marriage is enjoyed most when there is a mutual pursuit of peace. Plus, once you forgive each other, you get to make up, which is always fun. Then your body can return to a peaceful, conflict-free state and you can funnel the energy you were spending on being mad to better things. Have you ever noticed how your body feels when you and your spouse are fighting? It's one of the worst feelings, especially if you replay conversations in your head, thinking of better come-backs or alternate scenarios.

When your pride drops and your hearts turn toward each other, your physiology immediately responds and melts. Communicating from this place is more effective than in the heat of things. The sooner you are postured for forgiveness, the sooner your relationship will return to peace.

INVITE GOD INTO YOUR CONFLICT

There may be times when the solution or resolution to a particular conflict is beyond your capacity in the moment. Certain issues may call for counseling or a healthy outside perspective. We want to suggest in this critical time that you pause and sincerely invite God into the middle of your conflict.

It doesn't matter if it is a behavioral problem, heart issue, devastating news, grief, or long-term frustration. God is willing and able to help you navigate it. How does this look practically? You could read the Bible, listen to worship music, and monitor what you watch, read, or allow into your thought-life. Ask God to show you your part in the situation, the causes behind the issue so you can feel empathy and understanding, and the steps you can take to reconnect your hearts.

> THE SOONER YOU ARE POSTURED FOR FORGIVENESS, THE SOONER YOUR RELATIONSHIP WILL RETURN TO PEACE.

This may require some quiet time. Watch your words and be in listening mode. Be careful not to cement the situation with negative talk or a pessimistic outlook. Don't force your method of reflection on your spouse. Maybe they prefer a walk in the woods instead. If you decide to go to God before your spouse does, don't think it's a power play or an "I'm more spiritual than you" move. It is an act of humility. If you really want to be spiritual about it, it should be done privately so your pride can be excluded from the equation.

One of our favorite scriptures is Psalm 34:18: "*The Lord is close to the brokenhearted and saves those who are crushed in spirit.*"

He promises us His presence is in the midst of our troubles. This isn't a "when all else fails" option either. Practice making this one of the first things you do and see how differently *you* feel in the resolution process.

5

Helping Your Spouse Grow Out of Unhealthy Patterns

Notice we didn't call this chapter, "How to Change Your Spouse." We all know by now that the only person we can change is ourselves. Instead, we want to address our role in helping them overcome behaviors, habits, and beliefs that inhibit the life they want to live.

As caring partners, we need to gently let our spouses know about their "blind spots." Bringing these up may surprise them at first.

Perhaps your spouse does something that may cause them to not be received in the best way or tendencies that put their health at risk. We understand it takes guts to bring some things up, but no risk, no reward. The beauty of being their spouse is you get to see all 360 degrees of who they are. You can be the iron that sharpens iron, helping them become stronger and better. (See Proverbs 27:17.)

CLOAKED FEARS

Many times, unhealthy patterns stem from things that hurt us in our past and have somehow creeped into our present. They manifest in various ways and can often be misunderstood if we don't take the time to think and pray through where they came from. That's not to say we don't deal with them; it just means we extend grace to our spouse through the process of growing out of these patterns and behaviors.

As we share some of our issues, they may not be similar to yours. That's okay. They don't have to be identical for you to learn something from them. Hopefully, through these examples, you will be able to evaluate your own and experience breakthrough. Maybe there is a behavior you've been frustrated with in your spouse? It is worth examining the possible root issue so you both can approach it with eyes wide open. It's imperative to look past the surface layer to the emotion or fear it actually represents.

We were blown away when we discovered that despite our very different upbringings, we had the same top fear. This information is part of what allows us to deeply sympathize with each other and not violate those sensitive areas.

Some unhealthy patterns or behaviors are not straightforward in the beginning. In our experience, when we patiently asked God for insight into the issue, He was faithful to answer and reveal what we couldn't see in the immediate.

Our hope and prayer for this chapter, like the rest of this book, is that it helps you grow your love for one another and enrich your marriage so it can be a testimony and light to the world. It is likely that your spouse is sensitive about the patterns or behaviors you see, so they should be approached carefully and intentionally. We also suggest that you only deal with one issue at a time. You don't want your spouse to feel beyond repair because they are such a mess.

Charity

"WHAT? I SNORE?"

I remember the first time I told Ted that his snoring kept me awake most nights.

"What? I snore?"

No doubt he was shocked at the news, but once I had video footage of his chainsaw- bulldozer-esque snore, he was a believer. Thankfully, through the video and other episodes, we discovered Ted had a moderate case of sleep apnea and needed a CPAP (continuous positive airway pressure) machine. Had I never mentioned the snoring, his sleep apnea could have gone undiagnosed, leaving him at high risk for respiratory failure and death.

Early on in our marriage, I was quite abrasive. I had an opinion about everything and thought everyone should know it. Looking back, insecurity was very much at play during this season. Ted equated my words back then to an axe chopping things to bits. They weren't building or improving. They were just bludgeoning and destroying. In his mild manner, he helped me to see that most of the time, there was a better way to say the exact same things and I didn't always have to volunteer my opinion if it wasn't asked for.

What he was sharing with me in his own words is echoed throughout Proverbs.

Gracious words are a honeycomb, sweet to the soul and healing to the bones. (Proverbs 16:24)

I definitely could have been more gracious, but, honestly, until it was brought to my attention, I didn't know this was an issue. I didn't see it for myself.

Proverbs 3:7 says, *"Do not be wise in your own eyes."* Back then, I was only confident in the fact that I was smart. I wanted desperately to impress people and gain their approval. This method was exhausting and made everyone miserable. Reflecting on how much and how often I rattled off my rigid opinions makes me remorseful for who I hurt and sad that I carried so much insecurity. I wish I could have used what I had to love others and make friends instead.

I am so grateful for the love Ted has poured into me. Year after year, I feel my worth increasing, making me a better wife, mother, friend, business leader, speaker, and influencer. I am able to live from a place of having much grace extended to me and am able to offer it much more readily to myself and others. It's like being able to take a deep breath rather than feeling constricted and fighting for air.

Ted

FEAR OF BEING ALONE

The truth is, we all have things to work on at every stage of marriage. The better our relationship is, the better we become. This is a direct result of how much trust we have invested each other—trust that has been proven layer by layer, year after year.

Charity's main love language is quality time. In case I did not pick up on that fact, she made it very clear from the beginning that she needed face-to-face time, complete with conversation and connection. At the beginning of our marriage, I didn't have many friends, so giving her plenty of time was never a problem. Because we had recently relocated to Nashville, she didn't have many friends either and this was hard for a major extrovert like her. She loved being with her friends and got tons of energy from social gatherings. She lived in Dallas most of her life and had a plethora of meaningful friendships. But once we moved, it was just me.

The church we were attending at the time wasn't great at creating or developing community. And we were both working nearly all of the time so making friends was a challenge. Charity wanted me to make friends (at least in theory) probably more than I did at the time. Again, that's the way she's wired. But something confusing and frustrating would happen when opportunities arose. A couple of times when I wanted to play golf or hang out with some guys from work, I would ask her if it was okay and she'd say yes, but then start to cry.

What was I supposed to do? She wanted me to make friends, but fell apart at the idea of my spending time with them. Most of the time, I would end up saying no to the guys' invitation simply because I did not feel I could leave her like that. I also knew I need to figure out what was going on because this was not a healthy pattern.

Over time, I began to see that Charity had a hard time being alone. These feelings were compounded by a mild depression from stressful life events like her parents' divorce after twenty-five years of marriage, losing the house she grew up in, the 9/11 tragedy, moving to Nashville, struggling to find work, and getting married, all within a two-year time frame. That was a lot to go through and being alone seemed to make all of the stress very loud in her head.

Several conversations over the years allowed us to get to the root of her fear of being alone. Many times, she cried because she was embarrassed that she couldn't say the words, "Please don't leave me alone right now." She wasn't being duplicitous or controlling.

We both prefer to be together, but now, it is a blessing that Charity's fear of being alone has left as a result of prayer and healing. I'm thankful I was able to walk with her on that journey.

> WHEN YOU FIND ISSUES
> WITHIN YOUR SPOUSE,
> BE OPEN TO YOUR OWN ISSUES.
> YOUR SPOUSE ISN'T YOUR PROJECT
> AND ISN'T THE ONLY ONE WHO
> NEEDS WORK.

When you find issues within your spouse, be open to your own issues. Your spouse isn't your project and isn't the only one who needs work. Given time, your issues will surface as well. Together, you can conquer fears and eliminate the power that the past has over your present.

Charity

DISCOVERING MY PRINCE WAS FLAWED

It would be naïve of anyone to think that marriage doesn't require everything you have. I will be the first to admit that my expectations were set on the "better," "richer," and "health" portions of our vows rather than their negative counterparts. I was not one of those girls who planned and visualized their wedding day, complete with scrap books and fabric swatches. I didn't even know if I *would* wed. What I *did* know was that if a marriage was in my future, it would be to someone amazing. When Ted came along, I knew I could marry him because I thought he was pretty darn close to perfect.

Part of why I thought he was so amazing was because he still wanted to marry me, knowing all of that crazy stuff I shared with him on our first date. I knew I was smart, good with money, funny, and hard-working, but it felt like all of my good qualities were overshadowed by emotional issues and low self-esteem. I didn't feel worthy of love by someone so understanding and, in my eyes at the time, without flaw.

When I actually did have to face one of Ted's issues, it was hard on multiple levels. First, I had to acknowledge that he wasn't as perfect as I made him out to be in my mind. Second, he needed me just as much as I needed him. I didn't know if I was capable of helping him since the first several years were him helping me through my funk. This situation shifted me into a new and different role, which ultimately caused us both to grow.

BLAST FROM THE PAST

When Ted was a young boy, his mother was in a horrific car accident and spent months in the hospital. Ted's parents were already divorced by this time and her then-boyfriend was abusive to the boys, particularly Ted's brother. Once they told their father what was going on, he took the boys and had words with the ex and her boyfriend. Those two left town without looking back.

There was probably no easy way to explain her absence, but rather than telling the boys what really happened, Ted's dad said their mom's memory was damaged and she didn't remember them. This was easy to believe because the boys had already experienced things like her forgetting to pick them up after school. For thirty years, this was how "adult" Ted rationalized her absence.

In 2010, Ted began full-time nursing school. About a month after the semester started, I was in Phoenix visiting family when Ted called me. His voice sounded different. He said, "You'll never guess who called." This might sound awful, but because Ted's mom had been gone so long, the go-to answer for a question like this was always, "Your mom?" When he couldn't answer because his emotions were on overload, I realized this was a serious conversation so my sarcasm shifted quickly to sincerity. Then he said, yes, she had called him.

What in the world? She's been gone for thirty years and now, when I'm out of town, he's having this life-altering experience? Up until this moment, I never thought I would ever meet his mom much less get to know her. And her genes contributed to 25 percent of my children's DNA.

This unexpected reunion was so out of the blue and huge for our whole family, but very intense for Ted. We invited her to our home in Nashville so she could meet our kids and Ted could get some answers. It didn't take long for him to realize that what he had been told all of those years wasn't true. She remembered everything. And that stung deeply.

Despite the whole abandonment thing, she was a lovely woman and obviously in pain from guilt, shame, and regret. I wanted to lay into her and get some justice for Ted, but she kept crying grateful tears and it wasn't my issue, so I followed Ted's lead. Plus, I couldn't help but feel for her, too.

Again, "adult" Ted organized all the details in such a way that he was able to say that he understood her actions. I wasn't quite ready to sweep a thirty-year absence under the rug so easily. We spent several days getting to know her but not really pressing for answers to our long-held questions. Her heart could barely handle the overwhelming joy of the situation so we let that be the extent of the first visit.

We discussed some starter expectations with his mom and how to make her a part of our lives. Both of them would need new habits for this relationship to grow. Ted set the bar low so no one's feelings would get hurt between phone calls while they actually tried to remember to call each other. She went back home and we settled back into the routine of nursing school, the daily grind, and work.

Ted's semester continued on with a vengeance. I was already questioning if we as a family could survive the duration of nursing school if this was how hard life would be. The stress was mounting on all of us and I started to see a side of Ted I had never seen before. Up until this point, Ted was one of the most patient people I knew. He was an amazing father and consummate teacher to our children.

At this time, Luke, our oldest and only son, was five years old and all boy. He loved to be outside exploring the woods around the house, playing in the dried-up creek bed, and turning everything into a weapon to hunt whatever he was looking for that day. He and Ted had a very special relationship, but this season of life changed that.

THE SYMPTOMS OF DISTRESS

Things that our son would do or say that used to roll off of Ted's back were suddenly sending him into fits of yelling and anger. I would step in, look Ted in the eyes, and remind him that Luke was only five so Ted would snap out of it. These flare-ups were not constant or violent, but they concerned me because they did not represent the Ted I knew.

About a year later, I asked Luke to do something and he mouthed off with extra attitude. Ted was studying upstairs and could hear me getting worn out from holding my ground. I was doing my best to get Luke to straighten up and do what he was supposed to do, but it was a struggle. Ted being in school had made me the primary parent most of the time.

Like most concerned and compassionate partners would, Ted came down to take over like a relief pitcher because Luke was not responding to my correction. By this time, Ted had listened to enough of Luke's back talk and insubordination and was about to give Luke plenty to think about without taking time to cool off first. In my heart, I knew that nothing good would come of an experience like that so I literally got between the two of them and told Ted to stand down. He then tried to reach Luke. I had to put everything on the line and tell him that if he didn't back off, I was going to take the kids and leave.

I had never, ever had to risk our marriage like that before. Ted was agitated because he felt like I was defending our son's bad behavior when, in reality, I was protecting both of them. Ted stormed off to our bedroom and slammed the door. I looked Luke in the eyes and told him to go to his room and think about what just happened compared to what *could* have happened.

Then I cried, prayed, and reflected.

What had become of Ted's patience and mild manner? Was the stress of school too much? I was at a loss. After Ted had some time to cool down, I went and told him that I didn't think I was capable of helping him through this alone. I didn't have the answers he needed so I suggested he see a counselor immediately. I couldn't go on feeling like I might have to protect my son from my husband, both of whom I loved very much. I'm thankful for Ted's humility in this situation. He recognized that he wasn't behaving like himself and agreed to see someone who would work with our insurance's benefit of three covered sessions.

THE REVELATION

On the first visit, after asking some simple questions, the counselor pointed out something that now seems glaringly obvious yet it escaped us both at the time. Ted's anger wasn't from the stress of school or mouthy children; it was a manifestation of "child" Ted's deep pain from the conscious abandonment of his mother.

Her reintroduction into his life, coupled with Luke being about the same age Ted was when she left, created the perfect storm. Yes, school added to the pressure, but it masked the true issue. Looking back, I can see that anytime Luke pushed me too far, Ted's response was as if "child" Ted was saying, "Don't you make your mom so mad that she leaves us." It was his deepest pain mixed with his deepest fear.

If we had stopped at just the symptom, it would have seemed that Ted had an anger issue. The reality went much deeper. Anger is usually the result of unmet expectations. For years, Ted had believed that his mom left because she didn't remember him. Then he learned that wasn't the case at all.

While it hurt to watch Ted experience the pain of his mom being gone for thirty years and face facts that ripped his heart out, this was ultimately what brought the anger boiling to the surface.

The times spent with his mom since then are part of what will likely be a lifelong restoration process. There have been hard questions and feelings shared as both Ted and his mom navigate through the pain. We are so thankful she is a part of our lives now and glad our children will grow up knowing her.

These conversations, discoveries, and revelations came over an extended period of time with the help of prayer, counseling, and a commitment to helping each other make it to the other side. It may seem fast, neat, and tidy when it's typed out in a few short paragraphs, but the reality is that these paragraphs represent years of challenges that nearly brought us to our tipping point.

IN CASE OF EMERGENCY

It's imperative to know you don't have to navigate challenges alone. One of the things we did early on in our marriage—during a neutral, non-argumentative time—was agree on who we would go to in a time of marital conflict or an emergency, if we ever needed it. You can't make this kind of decision when emotions and thoughts are enflamed. One of you will think the counselor is biased and not be able to trust them or receive what's being said. Having a plan in place gave us both peace.

WHAT DOESN'T KILL YOU MAKES YOU STRONGER

Some situations fall into the category of crisis rather than conflict. This is where your commitment to each other is of highest value. You may think that some situations are beyond help, but if you show up for each other throughout the process, it deepens the love, trust, and connection you have.

In our years of marriage, we have seen couples buckle and split in times of crises. That doesn't have to be the case. Whether it's sickness, loss, unemployment, or something else acute and painful, your marriage *can* survive. Just because society says, "Bail if it gets too hard," doesn't mean you have to listen. Every marriage has difficult stuff. With both of us coming from numerous divorces, we have witnessed the threshold of what people can endure getting lower and lower with each divorce. What will it be next, the toilet seat issue? Control over the remote? Decide now to stand with your spouse through the hard stuff.

> DECIDE NOW TO STAND WITH YOUR SPOUSE THROUGH THE HARD STUFF.

Early on in our marriage, what we thought were marriage deal-breakers were based on fear, inexperience, and probably a dose of pride. Thinking that X, Y, or Z would be reason enough to give up on our marriage and each other seems so frivolous now. While we haven't experienced most of those things, we have seen some amazingly strong marriages around us work through issues like sex addiction, affairs, debilitating sickness, bankruptcy, and even the death of a child.

This showed us that what we thought would certainly destroy a marriage didn't necessarily have to. It also reminded us that we are all, at any given time, just a few decisions away from many of those things happening to us. It is with all humility and sobriety that we are here today sharing these things with you. We know marriage is a delicate balance. We respect the holistic gravity of our choices and offer our lives to God and say, "Here we are and here's our testimony."

WHEN GROWTH DOESN'T HAPPEN

We have also seen spouses who stood, endured, and believed for a marriage miracle that never came. The grief, heartbreak, and years spent waiting leave us all with questions. Much of it boils down to the other spouse being unwilling to do the hard stuff—the work that brings change, the honest conversations that open cans of worms, the counseling and accountability, the support and community, removing things in life that are a slippery slope back into bad habits, or distancing themselves from bad influences and relationships.

Marriage requires 100 percent from both of you and it's hard when only one of you is willing to put in the effort. It's not our place or desire to tell you what to do if this is your situation, but we would suggest first prayer, then counseling. Sometimes another person's perspective and insights can help both of you. Even if your spouse isn't willing to go, you can benefit from that support. Again, please don't stay in a situation if you are in danger.

WHAT YOU WATER, GROWS

If you are in process of working through an unhealthy habit or behavior in your spouse, understand the weight of your words.

Like water, our words can be used to cause good things to grow in them—or weeds. When we want to experience the best aspects of our spouse and help them quit bad habits, we need to build them up. Saying negative things can hurt them more deeply, for a longer time, than physical injury.

Speak to the growth and advances you see, even if they are small. Recognize and acknowledge the effort they are putting forth and celebrate them. Appreciate that they are probably scared they will let you down, regress, or even fail and they are trying anyway.

If you are the one who is going through the pain of change, while you may be nervous or agitated, especially if you are coming out of an addiction, please do not be ugly or curt to your spouse. Don't push their patience by demanding they accept whatever you spew at them while you are detoxing or trying to break free of bad habits. Stay humble and stay helpful.

Your spouse is just as concerned as you are and wants to be there for you. Don't constantly ask for space, giving them no idea where your head is at. Allow them into your thoughts and concerns. Let them speak to the courage in you and build you up. You don't have to go through this alone simply because it is your issue.

6

Family Values

Even before we said "I do," we were determined to have a different type of marriage than what we had witnessed. Yes, Charity's grandparents were positive role models, but we had to create some of the code ourselves; we had nothing to go on for the early years or raising children phases. Our vision was that we would be sickening love puppies, never to be shown up by newlyweds. We wanted to remain in our honeymoon mentality forever.

To keep our marriage ironclad, we had to establish what we actually wanted for it. This meant creating a plan with standards we wouldn't break. Yes, there were times when bending was necessary…but never breaking. We both saw—not only in our homes growing up but also in the world at large—that it was often repetitive little things that wore relationships down and eroded them. Over time, a constant drip can drill a hole into a rock. And so it is with simple irritations that break a marriage apart.

WHEN YOU STICK TO THE VALUES OF YOUR MARRIAGE, IT WILL HEAD IN THE DIRECTION YOU BOTH DESIRE.

When you stick to the values of your marriage, it will head in the direction you both desire. Values are guides for all major decisions, a hierarchy of things we seek to protect. It is imperative to be on the same page about your values. This often takes multiple conversations and sometimes years to tweak, but the outcome is worth it. It enables you to live as a cohesive couple and avoid unnecessary fights.

WE ARE A TEAM

The most intentional marriages always have strong teamwork. The couple is always reinforcing and building each other up. While growing up, both Charity and I were affected by the lack of teamwork in our parents' marriages. Because my biological mother left when I was six and my brother was four, my father worked hard to provide for us. He didn't like being single, so he married a woman with two children of her own. Then they had a child together.

Now, as a family of seven, our household expenses were dramatically higher—and wife number two didn't want to work. At all. She usually slept all day and was on the computer chatting most of the night. This put all of the responsibility of providing on my dad and much of the housework and cooking on me.

My dad worked three jobs to make ends meet for us. I hardly ever saw him and when I did, he was sleeping or resting. This made me very angry with my stepmom. Her laziness prevented me from spending time with my dad and for that reason, I was never going to marry someone who wouldn't work.

I wanted a partner, a teammate who knew and appreciated what it meant to earn a dollar. I wanted an independent woman, not someone living at home just waiting to get married and have someone else take care of her with no idea what things cost. I wanted a woman who was acquainted with what it takes to pay bills because I didn't want to be a dad who was gone all the time and never there for his kids. For me, a large part of teamwork meant we both work so we can both parent.

Charity

For me, being a team had a slightly different connotation. The only stereotype I was okay with at the beginning of our marriage was that husbands take out the trash. But beyond that, we would both cook, clean, earn a living, and have a say in how our money was spent.

I distinctly remember my mom being tucked away in our kitchen, cooking and preparing meals, while my dad was in the living room watching football in his leather wingback chair, directly below the air conditioning vent. I thought, *That will never be me. If meals are being cooked, we'll be cooking them together. If relaxing is happening, we'll be relaxing together.* My mom lived as a doormat for many years. This type of "women belong in the kitchen" model still happens in various social settings and I avoid it there, too.

For me, the idea of being teammates extends far beyond the kitchen. One of the main areas I was not about to tackle on my own was caring for children. Our firstborn was a test case that enabled me to study how Ted participated in a child's needs. Sure, he could not wait to bond with Luke, but what was life really going to be like when one of those 2 a.m. poopy diaper explosions or painful teething and crying spells came along?

About a week before Luke was born, I distinctly remember one of the best conversations Ted and I had. We were driving to our final appointment with the obstetrician when I looked over at him.

I said, "We are about to be very tired and very scared. We may even end up saying some things to each other that we don't mean. Can we just decide right now that we forgive each other and extend extra grace during this difficult time?"

He agreed wholeheartedly. We both knew we were in this together and were as ready as we could be to welcome our son.

Luke was due on July 3 and if he was late, induction was set for July 11, 2005. Since apparently I have what Ted calls a "penthouse womb," Luke had no intention of leaving his comfortable digs on his own. So with our doula, my mom, and all of my sisters in the hospital room on July 11, we began one of the longest days of my life.

My goal was to have a natural delivery, which meant everyone could be in the room when he was born. My dilation stalled after reaching four centimeters and then there was a concern over Luke's heart rate. I ended up having an emergency caesarean section after twelve hours of painful labor. Out of sheer exhaustion, I slept through most of the surgery. This wasn't the outcome we expected and it put me in a position of needing extra care and help that I wasn't ready for. I was prepared for being tired and discombobulated, but not fresh off the operating table.

From the very beginning, Ted was there for anything and everything I needed. The days my family had planned to spend helping out after Luke's birth were instead spent waiting or in the hospital while I recovered. I was devastated. Literally all of our plans and support went out the window before I was discharged. I didn't enjoy feeling physically limited and needing Ted's help just to go to the bathroom was both humbling and endearing. I was able to experience him as a true partner in a way that made me love him even more.

We were terrified when the hospital finally sent us home with this tiny stranger who needed everything from us. Didn't they know we had no idea what we were doing? In an instant, we were thrust into a deeper level as teammates.

The first night home with Luke was probably one of the scariest times in our lives. It had been a long time since either of us handled a baby. I had all sisters so a baby boy was new and unfamiliar terrain. But our house was more than ready. We had numerous diaper stations, complete with stacks of blankets, thermometers, burping cloths, and anything else we had been forewarned to have on hand. We read all the books and were ready to take on this first night...or so we thought.

After I nursed Luke, Ted changed his diaper, placed him in the bassinet next to our bed, and turned off the light. *Ahhhhh. We made it. We can sleep for a few hours until the next feeding.* Ten of the fastest minutes later, little Luke began to cry. Ted sprung out of bed like a gazelle and rushed to Luke's side.

I turned on the light and asked, "What's wrong? What does he need?" as if Ted could tell within three seconds of looking at him. His shocking response was, "I don't know." After a thorough examination, Ted discovered that Luke had peed through his pajamas. No problem. Each diaper station was equipped with multiple changes of pajamas so Ted put a fresh diaper on Luke, along with new pajamas, and changed out the wet blankets for dry ones. Crisis averted.

We got back into bed and turned off the lights. *Ahhhhhhh.* We were so proud of ourselves because look at us, we assessed our baby's needs and met them. A true parenting win. Forty minutes later, Luke started screaming. It was like the movie *Groundhog Day*. Luke had peed through another set of pajamas. I began to question Ted's diapering methods and this time took matters into my own hands. I switched diaper brands, put on his fresh diaper, fresh pajamas, and fresh blankets. We placed our precious little Luke back in the bassinet, got into bed, and turned off the lights.

No kidding, thirty minutes later, Luke was crying and had soaked through another set of pajamas and blankets.

"What in the world?" By this time, Ted and I were yelling out of exhaustion, frustration, and an underlying feeling of "maybe we are not cut out for this." Out of sheer desperation, I picked up the diaper package and began reading the information on it, looking for any clues that could help us figure out how to stop these leaks. I came across a tiny, yet essential detail about changing a boy's diaper that changed our lives. It said, "Point the penis down." Why did no one tell us this before now? Did they think we just knew what to do? Since that night, I have not seen those words on another package of diapers. It seemed as if that message was on *that* package just for us.

When he was home, Ted saw every diaper change as a chance to strengthen his bond with Luke and share the burden of his care. We had a beautiful routine for nighttime feedings. When Luke would stir, Ted would get up and bring him to me so I could nurse him. As most newborns are extremely sleepy, Ted would help me keep Luke awake so he would get a full feeding. When I was done, Ted would carry Luke to the changing station and talk to him while changing his diaper.

Ted never complained or said anything like, "I should be able to sleep because I'm the one who has to get up and go to work in the morning." He knew and appreciated that taking care of a baby all day long combined with surgery recovery was hard work, too, and happily partnered with me day and night. Needless to say, his teammate mentality made having children something I looked forward to each time.

------------------------------ *Ted* ------------------------------

OUR TIME IS OUR TREASURE

We place great value on our time together. Every decision we make for our family must filter through how it affects our time. Whether it's sports, lessons, church commitments, or friend time, it must balance with the amount of time Charity and I get to spend together. We have been married long enough to have seen some of our friends and family get divorced over issues that stem from too much time apart. I'm not even factoring in military deployments or job assignments that move one away for an extended period of time. Remaining a couple while not doing life together is nearly impossible and, for many, not desirable.

One of the slipperiest slopes that can lead to a passionless marriage is conflicting schedules. Charity and I have four children. In today's kid-centric society, it's easy to over-commit and have us going in opposite directions trying to get our kids to a bunch of activities. However, this divide-and-conquer approach is something we intentionally keep to a bare minimum. We don't want to spend time apart when we'd rather time together.

Our church in Nashville held a couples' fun night and invited the couple who had been married the longest to come forward for a game. The idea was for the spouses to guess what each other would say while sitting back to back. It didn't take a therapist to see that while they had many years under their belt, the love was gone. Not long afterward, that couple divorced. I'm sure both sides had their reasons, but what Charity and I observed was that they were hardly ever together.

So how can you evaluate if this is the case for you and your spouse? Here are some clues that might indicate you are spending too much time apart:

- Your extracurricular activities don't include your spouse.
- You don't know your spouse's favorite shows.
- You're not up-to-date on what activities energize your spouse.
- You couldn't even speculate about their immediate needs.
- You make plans without first running them by your spouse.
- You're not having sex very often.

Along with personal fulfillment, the main reason I went into nursing was for the opportunity to determine my own schedule. Charity shouldered so much of the family responsibility while I was in school that I needed to take some of that off her. Three days on with four days off flowed well with our values. Because Charity is an entrepreneur, she is usually able to flex her work hours around our family's needs. This fluid schedule gives us the privilege of meal planning, shopping, relaxing, and having fun together, building a stockpile of memories and experiences with each other. It allows our bond to grow even stronger because our hearts are in the same place.

> HOW YOU SPEND YOUR TIME SHOULD REFLECT WHAT YOU VALUE.

TIME FREEDOM

Time together is of high value to us, but so is time freedom. Part of what we love to do with our time is serve together. We look for opportunities that allow us to use our respective strengths in the same setting. There is nothing quite like having a "helper's high" together.

We also love to be hospitable. Nearly every week, we host a group of our friends at our house to have dinner and play games. This scratches both of our itches of friend-time and healthy competition. How you spend your time should reflect what you value.

Charity

We are not saying that every waking moment should be spent together sharing each other's air, but we *are* saying that time together needs to be a high priority. Time is our ultimate currency. You can never get it back once it's passed and there are no rollover minutes. Your spouse will either increase or decrease in value based on how they feel about the way you spend your time.

One of the most difficult things for me to hear from other women is how frustrated they are with their husbands yet they don't do him the honor of telling him the truth about what bothers them.

In our early years, especially before children, Ted and I would watch Dallas Cowboys games on TV together. It was nice because they are our favorite. All was fine until one game turned into two games and two games turned into an entire afternoon wasted watching football. I found myself bitter at Ted for him not seeing how watching football all day took away precious time that we could have spent in a way that actually benefitted our marriage. Ted's response was, "But we are together." This forced me to clarify what kind of time I was looking for. I didn't care for more time sitting side-by-side staring at the screen, watching games that didn't matter. I wanted to connect, which meant the TV needed to be off.

I asked Ted to compromise: no more than one game per weekend. He could pick the one that really mattered and we would watch it together. Then we would spend some time growing our relationship by doing something like going for a walk, talking, running errands, or even cleaning our apartment. Something productive! For a person who is as driven as I am, the non-productivity alone—just sitting and watching TV—drove me nuts sometimes.

Both husbands and wives can misappropriate time. Stereotypically, men might watch a ton of sports, play golf all the time, binge on video games, or go out for a beer every night after work. Women might enroll their kids in every activity possible, say yes to every party invitation, devote themselves to excessive "self-care" following two hours of spin classes or kick-boxing, and spend hours on social media. These things are not a problem in moderation. The problem is the more time you spend apart, the less your spouse will think that you value them.

BE UPFRONT AND HONEST *NOW*

The easiest way to make sure you and your spouse stay on the same page is to keep an open dialogue on where you both are at and be honest. What many find difficult to understand is how something that was once "okay" now bothers you. Do yourself and your spouse a favor and be honest about how their activities make you feel *now*, especially if they make you feel undervalued. Don't let things build up. Bitterness and resentment start off very small. We often minimize them because we don't want to seem petty. But over time, they can destroy a marriage from the inside out if not addressed in the moment.

Where you spend your time is an investment. The return on investing mutually in each other is exponential. Remember that your spouse is your primary account where you store life-long treasures. It is from this account that you draw upon especially during difficult seasons. You may have times when your spouse isn't your favorite person at the moment. For most couples, that's normal. We are human and we have the power to annoy each other. But having a deep well of investments from each other makes those brief moments bearable and passable. There will be many times when you need grace and mercy extended your way, so be sure to invest your treasure of time into your spouse.

MARRIAGE FIRST, KIDS SECOND

Creating a tiny person together can be a powerful source of connection, but they must be loved in the proper order. This can be difficult because their baby powers are significant. They come into the world all cute and cuddly, looking so fresh and innocent, then immediately begin to place huge demands on both of you. They make you tired, they cost money, they can't do anything for themselves, and, to top it off, they are a miracle and so precious. They are truly amazing and they draw us in.

Children have the uncanny ability to wrap us around their fingers if we aren't careful. But this isn't where their powers end. They don't know what they're doing right off the bat, but somehow, they discover the strategy of pitting parents against each other. From the very beginning, we decided our children came into *our* world, not us into theirs. We committed to always putting our marriage first above our children. As much as we loved them, they were going to move out after eighteen years or so—and we would still be married. Our plan was to be passionately in love even in the empty nest phase, not strangers who share a mailbox.

We've witnessed couples who overtly or covertly compete to "out-love" their children, vying to be the favorite parent. Your spouse should be the one receiving the lion's share of your attention, not your child. Children pick up on this. They realize they have power in this situation and they aren't afraid to wield it. They encourage the competitive environment by occasionally playing favorites or going from parent to parent until someone gives them what they want.

> PLAN TO BE PASSIONATELY IN LOVE EVEN IN THE EMPTY NEST PHASE, NOT STRANGERS WHO SHARE A MAILBOX.

Charity

BEING MARRIAGE-CENTRIC

It's easy to figure out if a couple is marriage-centric or kid-centric just by spending a little time with them. Our kids live in the healthy and thriving place of coming after our marriage. The other day when I asked my daughter Natalie what she thought I loved to do, she said, "Spend time with Daddy." She was exactly right.

We talk openly about our marriage being a priority with our kids because we want them to know that we intentionally choose each other first. We also tell them and show them that they are our very next priority.

DATE NIGHTS

We have always made date nights a part of our marriage. Having that time away, alone, not answering a thousand questions or feeling like you are in hostage negotiations over a piece of gum, is a nice break. Kids being kids, they used to try guilt us into staying home, as if somehow they were attention-deprived hatchlings. We would remind them that the purpose of these dates was to grow our love. Now that they are a little older, they are more than willing for us to "stay out as long as we need" so they can watch their shows.

Ted

When we were first talking about having children, I remember telling Charity, "Kids are aliens.… You never know what you're going to get." Children *are* an unknown. Each one comes with their own conditions, personality, and needs. I knew the best thing I could do for my children was to love Charity first and love her the most.

When I get home from work, my kids all run up to me to share their news, ask to go somewhere, or seek my help with something. Despite their noise and incessant demands, my priority is to connect with Charity first. I give her a hug, or a kiss if her hands are busy doing something, and see where she's at. To ensure my kids give me time to talk with their mom, I just start rattling off chores for them to do. That'll learn 'em. They watch as I make my way to her. I know it comforts them to know we are good and all is right in our world.

The role of a father has evolved. Rather than being disconnected workaholics, many fathers today are involved and engaged in their children's lives while a fair share of mothers have the opportunity to pursue careers and dreams. Some of the most well-tuned marriages are flexible and dynamic in that they can adapt to the various seasons of their family. Charity and I have gone back and forth many times on bread-winning, schooling, holding down the fort at home, and supporting the other during difficult times. Despite the undulation of life's demands, we make sure we are co-parenting as much as possible. One of the simplest ways to put your marriage first is to share the responsibilities and benefits of your children equally.

> ONE OF THE SIMPLEST WAYS TO PUT YOUR MARRIAGE FIRST IS TO SHARE THE RESPONSIBILITIES AND BENEFITS OF YOUR CHILDREN EQUALLY.

Our four children are experts at bargaining and negotiating. Of course, they have tried asking us both the same question separately to see who gives them the answer they want. But we keep our marriage first with our unified front. We do our best to never undermine each other because our kids shouldn't have that kind of power. After being together this long, we pretty much know how the other would answer most questions and requests. When in doubt, we check in.

If something happens where one of us has unknowingly gone against the other, we regroup and apologize, then deal with the child who has come to both of us in search of a certain answer. They know we don't allow that kind of behavior and we dish out consequences appropriate to the offense and offender. In simple terms, keep your marriage the main thing in your home. Your marriage is the foundation for your children's world. Keep it strong, unified, and together.

Charity

HEALTHY BOUNDARIES WITH FAMILY

An important dynamic to be aware of is the relationship your spouse will have with your family and vice versa. Since the goal is a healthy, thriving, and lifelong marriage, you need to appreciate the permanence of each other's family ties. Maybe you are one of the lucky ones who married into a great in-law situation where there's wonderful communication, joy, and love. Fantastic! You could probably skip this section if you want. However, the reality for most of us is that in some form or fashion, our families are crazy. So this is about managing that crazy with a solid helping of boundaries and protocols.

BOUNDARY 1: STARTING A NEW TREE

There is nothing more terrifying than the thought of repeating, reliving, continuing, or following the bad patterns, habits, or health issues of your family. Both Ted and I saw enough junk that it made us very cautious about marriage. Generational struggles that were present in our family trees—such as anger, infidelity, addiction, lack, abandonment, divorce, and depression—were all things we didn't want having any place in our relationship or home.

One day, I shared my sincere and painful concern with Ted: "What if I end up doing something awful like cheating on you because my dad cheated on my mom?" Or since we both have been abandoned by a parent, "What if I get to a place where I do the very thing I hate and abandon you?" In my mind at that time, I was the most likely to do this because Ted is so very loyal and doesn't like change. I, on the other hand, crave change, reinvention, and mixing things up because I don't want to get bored. Ted looked at me and could see the level of fear I had about hurting him and hurting myself. He said:

"We are a new tree."

We prayed right then and there to cut off the generational struggles and strongholds that worked to destroy both of our families. We also prayed for new things to come into our new family tree, like a lifelong love and marriage, trust, safety, provision, happiness, and lots of other good things. In all honesty, I believe God began this work in our lives. Yet at the same time, the enemy loves to talk so we continually remind ourselves of our new tree and the freedom it brings us. What *is* in our power is we can cast those fears away and keep ourselves away from any dangerous situations.

BOUNDARY 2: CLIMATE CONTROL

The spiritual climate of your home is worth fighting for. While a tense situation may appear to be about a physical issue, your heart can sense that what's going on is really spiritual in nature.

For example, after months and months of hard work, multiple jobs, saving up, calculations, and negotiations, we realized we had finally paid off the first $10,000 of our debt. It was a Friday night and we went out to our then-favorite restaurant for a modest celebration. We came home high on life and proud of ourselves. We felt so good, we decided to go through our stuff and get some donations ready for Goodwill the next day.

We woke up to an incomparable Saturday. The weather was breezy and beautiful, which made for a perfect "windows down" trip in Ted's truck to drop off the goods. The music was up, the wind was in our hair, and we were all smiles.

About halfway through our fifteen-minute drive, we were on the highway and suddenly began to hear very loud banging coming from under the hood. I don't know much about vehicles, but I could tell this sound wasn't good at all. Ted pretty much knew right away it was the engine rods trying to escape. I freaked out. When he said engine, I knew that meant big bucks.

I couldn't hold back the tears. How could this happen? We were working so hard and trying to do everything right to get our finances on track and then his engine goes? It felt like God was not protecting us, like we were being singled out and "taught a lesson" of some sort. I said, "Is this some kind of Job lesson, testing us to see how we will react?" I didn't want this kind of test, didn't ask for this kind of test, and I'm pretty sure that if it was a test, I failed. I was mad at God.

Sitting beside me in the truck, Ted was calm, cool, and collected. (This also made me mad.) He didn't join my freak-out session. Instead, he started praying and thanking God for the provision that was already on the way to take care of this situation. I thought, *Why couldn't I be more like Ted?* He was such a powerful example of trusting God. Instead of letting me jump off an emotional cliff, he set the spiritual climate to be one of hope and faith that we were about to experience a miracle.

Between a friend letting us borrow a truck for a month and an unexpected tax return, we were able to save up and pay for a $5,000 engine without going into more debt. What could have been disastrous ended up only being an inconvenience and a lesson in the benefits of spiritual climate control.

BOUNDARY 3: ALL IN THE FAMILY, BUT NOT IN THE LOOP

Another boundary that we set up was not sharing issues with our respective families. For example, we would not pick up the phone to tell our family about something our spouse said that hurt our feelings. This privacy and sanctity provided peace of mind for both of us. We knew that whatever we could and would quickly get over, family members would hold on to. We didn't want to give them any ammunition against our spouse or have them interfere with our marriage.

Family has a hard time getting over anything anyone ever did wrong to one of their own. They hold on to things in their minds forever. If you've ever crossed this line, you probably saw the doubt they had in your spouse the next time you were around them. They form their opinion of your spouse based on the information you give them. Unfortunately, bad things stand out more than good. Once they collect enough of these less-than-favorable bits of information, their instinct to protect their family member kicks in and they consciously or subconsciously begin trying to fray and dismantle the relationship.

After the doubt-filled looks come comments that question why you would ever be with your spouse. They will make passive-aggressive statements such as, "I never imagined you marrying someone so selfish," usually coupled with, "We wouldn't want another of those instances where you become hurt again." These little digs chip away at how you see your spouse. Worse, they are buried under the auspices of "caring" about you.

Simply put, keep family out of your relationship drama, but do share all of the amazing qualities you love about your spouse. Brag about how they care for you. Let your family see the brilliance you see so that their intentions will be to support your marriage rather than create tension and discord.

7

Money Matters

We all know money doesn't buy love or happiness, but it buys nearly everything else. It affects every area of our lives, including our health and well-being. Money must be managed or it will leave our hands for the next over-marketed product.

There is so much to learn about wisely handling money and it takes intentional information-gathering to learn most of it. It's even more complicated when two people from different backgrounds and money mind-sets come together and try to head in the same direction. American businessman and author Dave Ramsey once said at one of his live events, "When you agree upon your budget, you are agreeing upon your dreams."

Agreement is power. Without it, you will likely spend all of your energy battling each other rather than combining forces to move forward. When you talk and dream together, that synergy propels you forward exponentially and your vision becomes focused on your future.

Charity

A big source of financial conflict occurs when one person has one dream and their spouse has another. Be honest. If you are a bit of a "stuff" person, it's best to not represent yourself otherwise. Make your motivation clear rather than temporarily suppressing it with the random and painful binge spending. If you are a minimalist or a "fearfullist"—my own term for someone who's afraid to spend money they responsibly could—communicate that with your spouse so they can try to see things from your perspective. Just gaining a little understanding will aid in more productive money talks.

WHAT'S MINE IS YOURS

Ted and I used to be emphatic about couples sharing everything because that's how we do it and it feels great. We both have knowledge of and access to our money at all times. I still stand by this approach unless one partner has spending habits that endanger the financial security of the family or if there is some other crazy extenuating circumstance. Otherwise, there should be equal access to your money.

I can't tell you how many stay-at-home moms I've met who are only given access to what their husbands put into their "house" accounts. I'm sorry, but what era are we in? This communicates a lack of trust in her and her handling of finances, a lack of honor for the work she contributes to the family even though she doesn't receive a paycheck, and a spirit of control by only allowing her access to a small portion of the household income. The reverse may be true in a home with a stay-at-home dad. Money is an area that can bring immense unity between husband and wife when anchored with trust and honor.

> MONEY CAN BRING IMMENSE UNITY BETWEEN HUSBAND AND WIFE WHEN ANCHORED WITH TRUST AND HONOR.

Trust each other by giving full access and honor each other by not taking advantage of that access. On your wedding day, you decided you wanted to spend the rest of your life with your spouse, so you should have oodles of trust there.

I have taught my *Money Wise* course for over a decade and it always surprises me when I meet married couples who just can't imagine having a joint bank account. If you are in this group, I'm not bashing you, but I would like you to figure out where this mistrust or hesitation comes from. You may arrive at the root of the problem by honestly answering these questions:

+ Why *not* share one big pot?

+ What could happen that has you so concerned?

+ Is this a character issue in your spouse or in *you*?

+ What type of control do you think you need to have?

+ What kind of safety do you not feel if the money is shared?

If you do decide to go ahead and blend your finances, you can start slow. Set up healthy communication and ethics to keep unnecessary arguing at bay. Draft a monthly budget or spending map. You can find the details for a map in my book *Money Wise*.[2] This will help you both see clearly where your money needs to take you and what your options are for any overage. If you haven't already done so, discuss due dates for all of your bills and make sure balances are checked together beforehand to ensure they are covered.

Depending on your account balances, set a specific purchase amount for which you must consult each other before buying anything. Talk regularly about what expenses are on the horizon and the present state of your finances. Be mindful of larger purchases that may require some extra time, savings, or planning to acquire. Create your strategy together. Focus on how money makes you a team, not opponents.

WHO'S WINNING THE BREAD?

Over the years, we have flip-flopped several times on who was the chief breadwinner, but that never changed the fact that we are partners, equals, and peers. We don't outrank each other or take on a domineering attitude simply because one income is higher than the other. We both know what we add to our bottom line, on and off paper, and value all of it.

Having a higher income doesn't preclude one of us from contributing in all

> FOCUS ON HOW MONEY MAKES YOU A TEAM, NOT OPPONENTS.

2. http://www.charitybradshaw.com/resources/moneywise.

other areas of our household. There is no "lion's share" of housework going to the one who makes less, just as there is no shift in decision-making power or authority to the one making more. When it truly sinks in that *you are a team* and you are there for each other, the petty stuff stops. The only way we win is if we are both at the finish line together. We both carry all of the weight and share all of the reward.

For some couples we have walked with on this part of the journey, the breadwinner feels they are entitled to a higher percentage of the money than their spouse. It often goes unnoticed if the accounts are divided but rears its ugly head when it comes down to combining and sharing money.

Unless your spouse has given you some indication they cannot be trusted, this issue is likely rooted in you. We get it. We've seen other people take advantage of or wield control over their spouse and no one wants to be on the wrong end of that stick. But it is unfair to punish someone by treating them with distrust because of what you saw or experienced.

Charity

CO-CONTRIBUTORS

There are days when you couldn't pay me enough to deal with our children, days when inclement weather kept them home from school, days when we felt trapped inside, sick of each other, getting on each other's last nerve, fighting, dealing with who took one child's favorite whatever, who did whatever that hurt another child's feelings and now they're not best friends anymore—all of that kind of stuff. You just want to escape into a quiet room and not be bothered. But you can't.

Sure, no income was earned filling the glamorous role of parent, but much work was done. It would be insulting to treat that spouse as if they just "stayed home" all day doing nothing when in reality, they were on one of the most brutal yet meaningful frontlines ever. Ted and I both understand the effort and energy it takes to be the one championing the household because for us, it changes almost daily due to our schedules and the lines of work we are in. This allows for a constant flow of healthy respect for what we both do at work and at home.

Consider where you and your spouse are at on this issue. It may not be something you deal with now, but if it is, assess how you can begin to increase the honor you show your spouse no matter if they are the breadwinner or the CEO of the home. Appreciation is a major element, especially for those who don't go to a job where there are opportunities for recognition and acknowledgment. Vocalize what they mean to you and how you see all of their hard work and are grateful for it. It is because of the work they do for your family that you are able to be in the position of breadwinner in the first place.

COMPROMISE AND SPENDING MONEY

You may know someone who loves to "stimulate the economy" or "make it rain" by spending money at what seems to be a controversial pace. It's one thing if they are a friend, but quite another if we are married to them. The ones I know who embody this quality are generally very generous and love to see people excited when they give them gifts or do fun things with them. While much of that is enjoyable, it can also be dangerous to the bottom line.

If you are married to a "gifts" person—someone whose love language involves getting or giving gifts—you should set up a safe, healthy boundary amount for gift-giving. Over our marriage, there have been several times that Ted has wanted to give me something big or expensive and while I would very much enjoy the item, I didn't enjoy thinking about shelling out the money from our checking account to pay for it and disrupting our spending plan.

To satiate both of our needs, we budgeted a monthly "spending money" amount for both of us individually. We could spend the whole amount without having to explain how we spent it. Ted could spend it on barbequed ribs, flowers for me, toys for the kids, or whatever else he wished and I had no room to question it or be upset because it was already part of our household budget. If he wanted to get me something nice, he could simply save up for a few months and purchase it without creating waves in our account.

This budgeting concept offers peace-of-mind for cautious spenders like me and freedom to buy things for generous gift-givers like Ted. Whether your spouse is one way or the other, it's part of their makeup and giving them the ability to be themselves will make both of you happier.

Find that special amount your budget can handle and split it between the two of you. You may end up being the spouse who saves up for an all-inclusive anniversary vacation like I did because I didn't spend my money for nearly two years.

GETTING ON THE SAME PAGE

The blending of two money mind-sets often creates some of the most spectacular revisions for both people. For example, when Ted and I sat down to draft our very first budget just two tiny months after we were married, we quickly saw the disparity between our viewpoints. I was very cautious or "fearfullist" and considered this a healthy attitude above reproach. My reasons were:

+ I wasn't going to be dependent on anyone.

+ I saw the tension and stress money issues caused for my parents and didn't want that.

+ I knew money issues were the number one reason for divorce and I didn't want to be abandoned or alone over something as preventable as money issues.

+ Money protected me from certain pains so I didn't want to run out of it.

Ted had his own money issues and they were quite the opposite of mine. Because he had already experienced the weight of debt and had seen some provisional miracles, he trusted God and took a more laid-back approach. Here are my interpretations of his mind-set:

+ It feels good to give money away.

+ It's fun to buy Charity nice things.

+ There's nothing to worry about.

+ I will do whatever I have to do to provide for our needs, but God is our ultimate provider.

I might be slightly exaggerating Ted's issues but that's what they felt like to me. To find common ground between our mind-sets took months of work—years for some issues—before we arrived at an agreeable arrangement for both of us. My book *Money Wise* includes a "Financial Reality Check" tool that can help couples get on the same page.

The bigger picture in our story may help you sort out the money matters in your own marriage. If you zoom out from my issues, you can see that they were rooted in fear. I was treating money like it was more powerful than God, even though I was a believer and tithed my whole life.

I struggled with the overwhelming urge to insulate us with money. It manifested in strange ways. I never wanted to spend the money we were making. I wanted everything extra to go toward our debt or savings. I even became a black-belt couponer, something that took time and every bit of my brain power, just so we could stockpile supplies. It wasn't healthy.

But beyond spending, I really had a hard time being generous. I kept tabs on everyone, constantly checking to see if we were all equally contributing. It was painful. I didn't like the way stinginess felt, but it was almost a compulsion.

Ted modeled generosity from the onset of our relationship and I am happy to say that it has rubbed off on me. It *is* more blessed to give than receive and the feeling you get when you give makes you want to do it again.

Ted

DEBT WEIGHT

Growing up, money in our house had one choice and that was to meet our needs, not our wants. We rarely had any extra money. Although we never went hungry, we did stock up on microwave noodles. My dad worked multiple jobs simply to put a roof over our heads, clothes on our backs, and food on the table. We jumped from apartment to apartment, constantly chasing move-in specials. We never had a lot, but we had enough.

I watched my dad and developed a strong work ethic from seeing him sacrifice for any and all of our needs. This gave me a deep appreciation for him, yet made me hesitant to start a family. I thought I would work hard to make plenty of money for just me. I could buy myself nice things and "make up" for what I didn't have growing up.

This line of thinking led to some of the worst financial decisions I ever made. I had a job in management and was making decent money, but between my ignorance and predatory lending, I got into more debt than I could handle. I had a car I couldn't even afford the insurance on. What I didn't know sure hurt me and ended up hurting Charity, too.

I sort of adopted the mentality that more money equaled more problems. The pressure of my debt caused me to long for simpler times. The sheer magnitude of what I owed made me feel like paying it off was an impossibility. So, in my immature mind, I thought, "If I can't manage my money, why have it?"

Unfortunately, interest still accrued despite my change of heart. I wanted to escape the money rat race altogether. By the time I met Charity, all I had was an old truck, a home gym exercise machine, a small dresser, and a mattress on the floor in a friend's converted garage. The few clothing items I had Charity said were too small for me. On paper, I was a mess.

What this time showed me was compassion for others. I gave away Bibles, picked up cigarette butts, and even wrote Scripture verses on the back window of my truck. I was a radical, broke believer. I learned to trust God in my humbled state. I saw Him as my provider because I felt incapable of making good financial decisions. Therefore, I felt I had nothing to lose.

It wasn't until I met Charity that I really started to take action. I realized that with her, I did have something I could potentially lose. Being with her gave me hope to be a better man and money manager. I knew I needed to correct my behavior and grow my understanding of how money works. So I strategized a three-year plan to get out of debt before we got married.

Charity didn't want to wait three years and convinced me we could get out of debt faster together. Thankfully, she was already somewhat financially savvy. While she never carried debt before we were married, she knew she could help me figure out how to get out of debt sooner than my plan.

She was right. There, I said it. I'm glad she was, too. That meant three more years of wedded bliss because she was such a good saleswoman. When we married, I still had my debt and we committed the first years of our marriage to navigating out of it. This process empowered me to believe that God was faithful to provide.

These examples of God's provision led me to take the emotional power away from money. I somehow was able to figure out that money was a tool, nothing more. I made peace with the fact that money can come and go but what mattered would always be there. This peace is what I brought into our marriage and still carry to this day.

Maintaining a sense that money is not in control of your future is fundamental. When you relinquish control of your future to God, while doing what is in your power to do, money is simply a means to an end rather than a status level worth working yourself up over or a "get out of pain" card. Money gives you options but it should be regarded only as a vehicle not the driver. Remember, you and your spouse have both committed to do whatever it takes. Stand firm in your dedication and ride out the storms together.

One thing I've noticed is when one of us feels weak, the other is usually strong and able to offer encouragement. Charity and I have taken turns being strong for each other, knowing that feeling weak isn't the same as quitting or giving up.

Share your feelings. Pray about the situations that arise and walk every situation out with each other. There is something amazing about the view from the other side of a struggle when you are by each other's side looking back at what you've overcome together.

BOTH IN THE KNOW

While it is normal for one of you to be better with the details and management of your finances, both people need to be at the table for all money talks and decisions. If only one spouse makes all of the decisions and knows the status of the accounts, the other spouse is vulnerable—vulnerable to being blindsided, embezzlement, put in a precarious financial situation, and immense amounts of uncertainty and fear if anything were to happen to the spouse who did know it all.

Many of us have seen a new widow or widower who did not know anything about where their accounts are, how much is in them, who is owed money, what bills get paid when, and more. It is painful to watch and totally avoidable. There is nothing noble about being the sole financially responsible spouse. It is not serving your spouse to keep them out of the loop.

> HAVE A "JUST IN CASE" FILE READY AND GO OVER IT EVERY SO OFTEN TO KEEP BOTH OF YOU IN THE LOOP.

For this reason, Charity and I complied a "Just in Case" file that lists all financial accounts and their locations, insurance policies, go-to contacts, and other details should anything happen to one or both of us. This is also something that our children's godparents have knowledge of in case the need should ever arise. This file makes it easier to locate all monies and assets should a tragedy occur. Death or loss of mental capacity already places enough stress on a spouse without having to hunt for information, too. Have a "Just in Case" file ready and go over it every so often to keep both of you in the loop.

Charity

This organization and conversation is really a gift to your marriage. Yes, it's hard to even think about the possibility of losing your spouse, but preparation is necessary.

In fact, Ted and I recently met with our financial planner. It never fails to take my breath away when I see the page where it speculates our "anticipated end of benefit" and lists the year they think we will die based on statistical analysis. Of course, I know it's only a guess, but it sure is sobering and reminds me to appreciate the time we have together. Ted has always said we're going to live to a hundred and twenty. We'll see.

———————————————— *Ted* ————————————————

GENEROSITY

One of the best things Charity and I did was get on the same page when it came to giving. We both were already consistent tithers at church, but generosity extends far beyond those four walls. One thing I have always loved about Charity is that she is a good friend. This was one of the top qualities I looked for and I was excited Charity already had it going on. She takes good care of her friends and people God points out to her. To me, this is an extension of her generosity.

When we were first married, she was operating from a place of self-preservation. I have seen God provide through some of the hardest times financially and I know we can survive much more than our minds can imagine so I don't worry as much. This frustrated Charity at the beginning because I think she wanted me to join her in her worry. She would get mad because I wasn't as "concerned" as she was about the account balances. I wasn't doing anything to make the balances worse so what good would worrying do? None.

While we were in the middle of working our two or three jobs to get out of debt, God would present opportunities for us to give to others in need or bless someone. I remember our church at the time gave us the opportunity to support missionaries on a monthly basis. Charity and I came up with an amount we wanted to give to the missionaries rather than put toward our debt.

This opportunity to give in the middle of our own needs helped Charity step out further in trusting God with our finances and our family. This act of faith drew us closer together and collectively closer in our relationship with God. It wasn't just the two of us trying to make this thing work alone; we had a partner in God and that was better than any amount of money.

Charity

I have always loved Ted's generosity. He is truly not controlled by money or unnecessarily concerned about it. His modeling this faith-filled life has stretched me way further than I could have accomplished on my own. I vividly remember the missionary support opportunity Ted mentioned because when we talked about it, I said one amount and Ted's was more than double mine. This made me feel like a horrible person, yet I also thought he was crazy and a little out of touch with our situation.

In reality, both amounts reflected our individual mind-sets around money and provided another indication of how much we needed each other for balance. We work best together. With the understanding of how each other works, our numbers get closer together the longer we're married. I've learned to stretch, he's learned to rein it in, and it keeps getting better.

Because this is an area I continually strive to grow in, I look for opportunities to bless someone as I feel it impressed upon my heart. I know the value of sowing into the lives of others and how it always returns at just the right time. Ted and I have a threshold where we know we need to consult with the other person on spending and even giving, but when it's under that amount, I still love letting him know about the seeds of generosity we are planting. I can see the happiness it brings him for me to walk in this new level of freedom and faith, not to mention the divine blessings that follow generosity.

Generosity involves more than money. We can be generous with our time and talents as well. There have been times when Ted would pull his truck over to help a stalled car through an intersection. I've helped a single grandmother who was struggling to mow her lawn. From painting, landscaping, hurricane and flood relief, bags of food for hungry kids, meals for recovering or grieving friends, cleaning, babysitting, and more, we've done it all and recommend you jump on in. Being generous together feels amazing.

If you are struggling financially, generosity changes the dialogue of your home, shifting your perspective and bringing joy. Many times, this is the best medicine during hard times because it takes your focus off the problems and on to how you pressed through together. In our lives, God has often used people to bless us when we were struggling. When He places it on our hearts to do something for someone, it's because He wants to use us to be the hands and feet that deliver what He has for them.

> IF YOU ARE STRUGGLING FINANCIALLY, GENEROSITY CHANGES THE DIALOGUE OF YOUR HOME, SHIFTING YOUR PERSPECTIVE AND BRINGING JOY.

While money issues can destroy a marriage, much good can come from allowing your finances to be a unifying force for you. Get on the same page with your budget. Honor each other in the way you handle it. Be generous. Plan for the future and live well in the present. With these tenets in place, you will find that money isn't anything you need to fight over.

8

Sexpectations & Intimacy

Let's not kid ourselves, sex in marriage is ~~a gift, a labyrinth, a roller coaster~~...an area we all would like to make sure is working well that's rewarding for both.

As much as it is romantically fantasized about and neatly polished in movies, books, or even our own minds, the real thing in real time takes patience, practice, and much communication. One thing is certain: there are no real "sexperts" who know what will work for *you*.

You and your spouse are a unique combination of feelings, experiences, and preferences. It's okay for there to be differences of opinion on this topic. It has been our experience that couples who are sexually satisfied are less grumpy and more fun to be around.

We are bringing it up here because we want to do whatever we can to make this world a better place, one happy couple at a time.

Ted

DON'T BELIEVE THE LIES

I didn't know what to expect. Looking back, I set the bar so low that disappointment was nearly impossible. In fact, I remember thinking before we were married that even if Charity never said she loved me again, I would still love her and still stay married to her. Part of this was rooted in my fear of abandonment and part from watching my dad stay loyal to a cheating step-mom for years. My overall impression about sex in marriage came from the general consensus of married guys I knew: at best, it was sporadic.

Before I met Charity, I imagined that once a woman got her ring, the man was trapped and sex dried up quicker than a puddle in Texas heat. On the other hand, I knew Charity was a preacher's kid and I heard good things about what that meant. So I hoped for the best.

Going into marriage with all of this confusing information, I was pleasantly surprised by our openness, fun, and frequency. I realized I had believed a long-held lie that marriage was confining, sex-less, and boring. It made me question what other lies about marriage I had been believing because what we were experiencing was far from all of those things.

We were having fun and it made me feel desirable. I never thought I was good looking or even noticeable, really, so to go from that to having someone rip my clothes off every time I walked through the door did wonders for my confidence.

Marriage was also exciting for me because I was ready to give good lovin'. Half of the magic of sex with your spouse is figuring out what makes them crazy and then doing it well. I was ready and willing to meet Charity's needs and she felt the same way.

For many relationships, sex doesn't feel mutually beneficial because one spouse may be less concerned about the other's needs. I am here to tell you, when you both own the fact that you have the privilege of being everything to each other sexually, *giving* to them is going to come back full circle in the way they love you. You will reap the benefits! A partner who is fulfilled sexually will want to participate more often. So focus your efforts on your spouse first.

Charity

IT'S NOT A COMPETITION

Before we were married, Ted and I took some time to discuss what we thought we would be comfortable with, along with any boundaries or reservations we had. We were able to create a buffet of things that worked for both of us. Like many in the honeymoon phase, we put in the effort with lingerie, candles, music, frequent showering, shaving, perfumes, and colognes. You know the drill— whatever it takes to make those moments *perfect*.

I'm not sure if Ted was as concerned as I was, but I felt like I had to compete with the whole world of women for his attention. To be clear, he did not make me feel that way. Society did. Sadly, just walking through the mall these days is a hyper-sexual experience. I was determined I was going to be Ted's dream girl and that meant not letting him leave home with any need unmet.

My motto as a "good wife" and fellow sex enthusiast was to give Ted as much sex as he could handle the first year. In fact, I regularly give this advice to engaged couples because there are so few distractions in the beginning that you both can work out the kinks and become champs at pleasing each other sooner rather than later. I'm glad I did. It built a very strong bond between us.

It increased our self-esteems as we embraced being each other's ultimate friend with benefits.

I wanted Ted to trust that I was not going to starve him sexually and there would not be a scarcity issue that caused him to panic or be agitated. Since we agreed we would forsake all others and not cheat on each other, I figured I better hold up my end of the deal by giving him somewhere to go with all of his needs. While I didn't "need" sex as much as he did, it was still mutually beneficial.

GET HER MOTOR RUNNING

Creating intimate environments paved the way for many of our best conversations, allowing our hearts to grow closer while being physically close. Sex and intimacy are tenuously related. As wives, we want the heart connection first. This warms us up to the idea of being physically available.

For many women, stirring up the sexual appetite starts in the mind. This is a huge piece of valuable information for you husbands out there. If you want a wild romp around some time in the near future, begin peppering her with verbal teasers about your desires and then wait. Let the tension build and let her think about all of the ideas you dropped into her head. Kiss her. Take some of the burdens off of her plate so she can feel your concern for her and awareness of all she does.

Set the atmosphere. If you are in the pre-kids phase, this doesn't take as much planning, so make good use of the time. If you have kids, do your best to get them situated for the time you need. Prepare the bedroom in a way that shows her you want to take care of her needs first. I am a sucker for a good massage. Maybe your wife is too? Help her strip away the excuses or reasons that might keep her from joining you in some afternoon delight or midnight madness. Let intimacy pave the way to amazing sex.

For our first anniversary, we were not rolling in the dough so we had to be creative with our gift ideas. Ted made a three-ring binder that held several pages of "coupons" I could cash in whenever I wanted. From foot rubs to fantasy, the coupons had me covered. While I knew Ted would always "get his," it was nice to feel his heart to tend to my needs and desires.

One thing I really enjoyed was watching Ted blush, smile, and flex his muscles whenever I told him how sexy he was to me. It was like watering a plant. He just perked right up every time. He thrives on feeling desired and I am happy to help him flourish. Ladies, just as much as we wives want to be the object of our husband's affection, our husbands want to be desired by us. They want to know we are into them like catnip. Sex is one of the most efficient and effective ways to communicate this to them. They read this memo loud and clear.

LET INTIMACY PAVE THE WAY TO AMAZING SEX.

As newlyweds, sexy time was not complicated. We didn't have kids and everything they entail. We didn't have a ton of friends since we had just moved to a new city. Plus, we didn't have family nearby meddling in our business. So when we weren't working our numerous jobs, we were making good use of our time. We both worked close to our apartment, so "nooners" were a big thing. If you are in the newlywed season, here is one of the best pieces of advice we can give you: make love often.

Protect and reserve energy and time for sex. Don't always make it a nighttime thing either. If you have an evening out or date night planned, have sex before you go out. This way, you aren't full from dinner or tired from the day's activities and you've burned some extra calories. Bonus!

SNACKS, DINNERS, AND FEASTS

Not every sexual encounter has to be the same. In fact, variety can be the spice of your sex life, too. One of our favorite analogies that addresses some of the options is the idea of snacks, dinners, and feasts.

Since this is an appetite we are talking about, there are times when just a little something will do to tide it over. Sometimes, it's famished and needs a four-course meal. This concept helped Ted and I get on the same page for both of our points of view. While I may not be able to fully sympathize with a man's frequent need for release, it is something I know about and therefore don't ignore or begrudge.

SNACKS

Sex may be the furthest thing from my mind, but if I see Ted is getting a wee bit crunchy or cranky, I know it may be time for a "snack." A snack is basically a quickie that helps him unwind and de-stress. This is as much a need for him as a love note is for me. This may be a revelation for some women, but a husband's need for sex is not immature, shallow, wrong, or unhealthy. They are *wired differently*. Sex is how husbands get that connected feeling. They are designed to crave sex as part of God's plan for keeping the human race alive.

Snacks are a great precursor to anything that may involve patience or endurance on the husband's part. If there is a long day of chores, kids' activities, Christmas decorating, or tax preparations, where you and your husband will be stretched thin, pay it forward and give him a snack. I promise, it helps. You are doing yourself a favor by doing him a favor. Make it totally spontaneous and radically fast. This is one case where a little goes a long way.

DINNERS

Dinners are when you have a little bit more time to let things develop. They are mutually beneficial and both spouses should take turns initiating at this level. These longer encounters strengthen sexual attraction and connection. They provide time and space for foreplay, fine-tuning techniques, and giving both partners a chance to be fulfilled.

We're not here to preach numbers or specify frequency, but these should be as regular as you can make them because they are a priority. These should be a staple, not a special occasion. Don't rush. Use this as an opportunity to explore something new. Be sure to get the mind and body involved.

FEASTS

Feasts are decadent, memorable encounters. They are definitely mutually beneficial and usually talked about for years. Feasts are more than sex because they nourish parts of you that you never knew needed nourishing. They thrive on interruption-free time that has been set aside specifically for mutual pleasure.

Nowadays, with four busy kids, a feast time could occur when they're all at school or at friends' houses. It may be when we take a vacation or weekend getaway to grow our love. I'm a firm believer that the beach is sexually inspiring because it melts my stress away. It literally is my favorite place on earth to go with Ted. Our long-term plan is to go as often as we can.

Take pride in taking care of your spouse sexually. Appreciate the gravity of monogamy and the privilege of being the one your spouse has committed themselves to exclusively. Do not starve them or make them beg. Leave no room for temptation by keeping them fully satisfied.

NEVER FAKE IT

We all know we shouldn't lie, but marriage presents some gray areas. When it comes to not wanting to hurt our spouse's feelings, it's easy to "take one for the team" and fake enjoyment. However, over time, faking becomes exhausting and turns into a big heaping pile of regret.

When Ted and I were discussing marriage, I didn't know what to expect as far as my own sexual fulfillment was concerned. In my mind, sex always seemed to favor men and women got the short end of the stick. I knew Ted would not have any problems is the orgasm department, but between all of the magazine articles, books, and chatter, the prognosis wasn't very favorable for me as a woman. I heard plenty of negative messages like, "It hurts," "You won't like it," "I can't wait for it to be over," and "It's all he thinks about."

When I was growing up, sex wasn't a regular topic at our house. My mom was a virgin when she married and didn't have extensive experience or information to help me feel confident about my sex life. While she was very open about the science of sex, there wasn't much depth after that. In my mind, initially, sex was something I would engage in for my husband rather than for both of us.

The hit movie *When Harry Met Sally* came out when I was in my early teens. The infamous scene where Meg Ryan fakes an orgasm made us all laugh to the point of tears. But afterward, many husbands were left wondering if their wives were faking orgasms and if they could tell the difference between real and fake.

Whether we want to admit it or not faking an orgasm is a form of lying. Some have been doing this kind of lying for years and have no idea how to begin to be truthful. At the beginning of our marriage, one of the things I told Ted was that I would never fake an orgasm. I wanted him to be able to trust me and know that whatever he was doing was either working or not working. I also wanted to have the real deal.

Since men are creatures of habit, I knew that if I faked an orgasm, he would keep doing...whatever. If a man thinks he's doing something right, he will keep on doing it. Faking it would seal my fate in the sexual fulfillment department. It would ensure that I would never have real orgasms. And Ted would be hurt when the truth finally came out.

If you have been faking it, an honest conversation is the first step. Yes, it may be difficult. But this is a great opportunity to show vulnerability and personal growth, along with a desire for a better sexual experience for both of you. Just the fact that you are reading this book in an effort to have the best marriage possible is a great way to start the discussion. Your intentions may have been good in the beginning—you wanted him to feel good about himself—but faking it has left you unfulfilled. It's hard to make a course adjustment but not impossible.

> **WHETHER WE WANT TO ADMIT IT OR NOT, FAKING AN ORGASM IS A FORM OF LYING.**

As with any conversation of this magnitude and fragility, timing is everything. We don't suggest having this discussion in your bedroom but rather on the couch or the backyard patio, someplace neutral and relaxed. Own your part in the issue. Express your desire for him and commitment to better communicate what you need, what you like, and what really works. Make room for several possible reactions and don't push him for immediate forgiveness.

It may take some time to process, depending on how long this has been going on.

HURDLES

There have been times when sex was a challenge for us and we are sharing these things so you will know you are not alone. While we can't speak to every issue that could possibly come up, we can share the ones we've gone through. Too many things go undiscussed, leaving people feeling like something is wrong with them. We want to pull back some of the curtains.

Ted

CHILDHOOD SEXUAL ABUSE

One of the issues we had to deal with was past sexual abuse. I was victimized by a female relative for several years, starting around age nine. This distorted my view of sex and its purpose early on to be something that was solely physical with no connection or even acknowledgement of the relationship or what was happening. Plus, being so young, I didn't know what to do with the feelings and ended up processing most of them as anger.

It wasn't something I thought to mention to Charity right away because I had put it so far out of my mind, but as time passed and conversations took place, I shared what happened. When the memories flashed back, I didn't try to hide them. I am so thankful Charity was a safe place to go with the pain of the abuse and anger from the circumstances that led up to me being in such a vulnerable place. I didn't realize my feelings about what happened were so strong and so stifled until I started talking about them.

It certainly wasn't easy for Charity to hear what happened. Like any of us, she wished she could have been there to defend me from such horrible things. She wished she could take the pain from me and exchange the memories for innocence. Charity helps other authors and sadly, many have a history of sexual abuse or rape. I don't believe this is anything new; it's just being talked about more.

Allowing your spouse to know your full history helps them understand your behavior better and helps you to feel loved completely. Abuse tends to make some feel dirty or unworthy of a healthy relationship. This distorted perception of self-worth can negatively affect relationships if not dealt with and restored. We're not saying you have to share everything all at once, but begin where you can with what you can and ask your partner for patience.

If you are the one hearing this news, do not re-victimize your spouse by asking questions like "Why didn't you…?" or "What made you think…?" It is already a huge step for them to open up about their deepest pains so be there to comfort and love them through the journey to complete healing.

Charity

WHEN SEX IS PAINFUL

Right around my twenty-eighth birthday, Ted and I both decided we were ready to become parents. Immediately, it was game on. We were having sex all the time. I was excited because this was now sex on a mission. We were going to make a beautiful baby and it was going to be great. This was about two and a half years into our marriage, so by this time, we felt like we knew what we were doing. Although Ted tried to say, "We could always use more practice."

Two short weeks later, it was Halloween and I was exhausted, which we learned was the first clue my oven was on. One digital pregnancy test later, we found out we were expecting. That was fast! I broke out in hives, looking at the test and thinking about how this baby was real and eventually would need to exit my body and oh, my gosh, labor, delivery, sleepless nights...it all started swirling in my head. Once the hives settled down, I was able to join Ted in the excitement, especially since this was the first grandchild on my side.

About a month or so into the pregnancy, sex began to be painful. There was no fear of it hurting the baby or anything like that and no lack of lubrication. It just hurt, every time. Ted couldn't stand the thought of hurting me so he stopped expressing any needs. I would still try to rally, only to end up in tears from the pain. My obstetrician was no help; she said I needed to switch lubricants, which we had already tried several times.

The rest of the pregnancy went by with no improvement. I had friends who had the best sex of their lives while pregnant. They were having so much fun and yet I was in agony. I was jealous of them and definitely felt I was dealt a crap hand. Even though I planned and prepared for an all-natural birth, I ended up with a C-section. In a way, it was a relief because I didn't experience the horrors of cutting or tearing, which I just knew would make matters worse.

The pain continued through breastfeeding. By this point, I was terrified I would never enjoy sex again. I was devastated and depressed because sex was definitely a highlight of our lives. I felt broken and ashamed. Everyone tried to make me feel like I just needed to relax. Folks, this was not a relaxation issue. I tried everything from a glass of wine to deep breathing on top of just wanting to be intimate with Ted. Something was physically off.

Just a week or so after I stopped breastfeeding, the pain began to subside. Of course, we were both still a little nervous, but the worst was over...at least until the next pregnancy. After doing some research and asking around, I found out there was a medical explanation. Nothing was "wrong" with me. I was just one of the unlucky ones who had a hormonal issue.

I can't explain how grateful I am for Ted's unwavering support during this time. He never made me feel bad, never pressured me, and never made me feel he would go outside of our marriage because I couldn't enjoy sex. We did become very creative during this time and were less concerned about formalities in order to maintain our desired level of activity. The fact that Ted loved my pregnant belly made this time very special despite our issues. He made me feel amazing by hugging and rubbing my growing baby bump. As each pregnancy progressed and baby bump grew, he looked more and more proud because he "did this to me."

By the time we had our fourth and final child, we knew the routine and didn't worry about when things would be back to normal. We didn't try to rush the process and kept the creative stuff going. Marriage isn't a sprint and while sex is a great benefit, it isn't everything.

> MARRIAGE ISN'T A SPRINT AND WHILE SEX IS A GREAT BENEFIT, IT ISN'T EVERYTHING.

With each child, Ted took better care of me. My love for him grew and I felt more valued each time. If you take on the belief system that marriage is about serving each other, the sex part is simply an overflow of a full heart. You two can climb any mountain together.

FLUCTUATING LIBIDO

Unfortunately, there isn't a visible gauge or meter for one's sex drive. Most of us aren't fully aware of the moving parts or contributing factors that produce a healthy one either. Between stress, having babies, aging (ugh), and other factors, libido can go all over the place, including away. It's easy to mistakenly think it's an attraction issue rather than an interruption caused by changes in your body.

I am very sensitive and aware of my feelings, and I also pay attention to my body more these days. One of the things I noticed about a year ago was I had little to no thought of sex and had very little energy. Previously, even on my busiest days as a mom and entrepreneur, I usually had some flicker of desire for sex, but even that seemed to be gone. I felt numb or neutral. Sex wasn't even something on my radar—and that scared me.

> WHEN YOU HIDE SEXUAL DYSFUNCTION OR RELATED PROBLEMS, YOU WILL NEVER REACH A SOLUTION.

I normally initiated sex at least half of the time so to go from there to not even thinking about it was a dramatic shift. I felt horrible. *Was I bored sexually? No longer attracted to Ted?* The last thing I ever wanted to do was to look outside of our marriage to get my needs met. I felt guilty and scared. There's not enough discussion about this type of stuff.

At one point, my physical energy had dropped so low that even lifting my arms exhausted me. I woke up wanting to go back to sleep and with four kids and a business, that was impossible. I reached out to my sister, Dr. Spice Lussier, who runs a very successful naturopathic medical practice. I told her what was going on and scheduled a trip to see her, get some blood tests, and have her help me figure out how to feel better.

It's amazing how you can feel better just by knowing what's wrong. I am a huge advocate for being informed about your health and encourage you to get bloodwork done regularly. The lab tests showed that I needed additional thyroid support and more iron, plus my testosterone level was low.

This was common among women my age. Most men and many women are running around low on testosterone. This affects their energy levels, joints, metabolism, sex drive, and more. Most men are told as long as they have sex on the brain occasionally and can get an erection, they're fine. But that isn't necessarily the truth. Plus, there is a huge gap between "normal" range and optimal.

I started to take the necessary supplements and was treated with a pellet that delivers slow-releasing doses of bio-identical testosterone. What a difference! I felt like myself again—maybe even better—which was an answer to prayer.

This is a prime example of a situation that would not have caused as much emotional pain had it been an open topic of discussion rather than taboo. If you are experiencing these or other issues, know that, first, you are not alone, and second, ask for help. When you hide sexual dysfunction or related problems, you will never reach a solution.

Look for answers. If the first doctor looks at you like you have two heads, move on to the next. Maybe even ask a friend who's been married a while if they or anyone they know has been through something similar. Half of the solution is simply finding out you're not the only one with this issue.

INTIMACY

From the beginning, both of us pressed into intimacy. Over time, the outcome of this all-in approach was a steady lowering of inhibitions, setting the stage for some of the deepest discussions we ever had.

Intimacy occurs in the atmosphere of trust and builds layer by layer. We slowly uncover our vulnerabilities, carefully placing them in each other's hands, watching and making sure they are handled with care. Intimacy is the secret place of marriage, the axis from which everything else radiates. The more points you are able to place in your spouse's care, the stronger the axis becomes. The stronger the axis, the better able you are as a couple to handle challenges.

THE BONDS OF MARRIAGE AREN'T A SINGLE LINK BUT THOUSANDS OF TINY STRANDS OF INTIMACY THAT INTERLOCK AND STRENGTHEN WITH EACH CONNECTION.

In marriage, sex and intimacy are symbiotic; they work powerfully together. It's healthy and normal for one partner to desire sex more and the other to desire intimacy more. However, the goal is to allow each other's preference to increase in importance in our lives as we celebrate our love for them and how they bring balance to us.

We need both sex and intimacy. Having a partner with a different priority can only benefit us. If sex was everyone's priority, nothing would get done in this world. If intimacy was, no babies would be made and we would go extinct. We need each other.

Intimacy is the long-term investment strategy for marriage. It is making space for us to reveal the sacred parts of our heart and share things no one else knows about us. It creates powerful magnetism and expands trust. The bonds of marriage aren't a single link but thousands of tiny strands of intimacy that interlock and strengthen with each connection.

Intimacy can be shared by a simple look across a busy kitchen, conveying gratitude, desire, commitment, or even a mutual disdain for the momentary chaos. It can be a long embrace where you feel like you are melting into one person. Intimacy is the quiet space for the deepest parts of us to come out. It is the glue during difficult times or tragedies. It is nourishment for the heart of your marriage and probably the single most vital factor outside of God.

Intimacy needs time, space, and intentional surrender of our schedules, agendas, and to-do lists. We exercise listening to understand, empathy, grace, and acceptance to envelope our spouse in love. When your spouse shares something painful or shameful from their past, place yourself in their shoes. Feel what they felt and attempt to see through their eyes. Remind them of who they are today and how much they mean to you. Revealing those wounds can make them feel nervous and vulnerable, so be sure to reinforce your love and appreciation for them and how far they've come.

It's okay to cry and grieve over something your spouse has been through. Share the burden, even for a moment, to allow them to feel their pain is finally being acknowledged, validating their wounds. Intimacy says, "I see you. I see your pain, your past, and your present—and I love you all the more. Thank you for sharing this with me. I know it was difficult and I'm sorry you had to experience these things." Intimacy doesn't try to right wrongs; it simply listens and acknowledges.

There are times when your spouse might share something that does need additional support or counseling. This requires a huge amount of courage and trust on their part so be gentle and patient in the process.

Through intimacy, we are privileged to be part of the soul-healing and nurturing of our spouse. It is a tremendous honor not to be taken lightly. Remember, they are your biggest investment, love for a lifetime, best friend, and co-captain on this ride of life. What you give in intimacy will come back to you in love.

9

Marriage Models

Our culture works very hard to dictate what it wants us to value. From moral standards to consumerism, the external pressure is real and constant. To live outside of this "norm" takes intentional thought and commitment.

Marriages are under scrutiny on all sides. Either it's got to be perfect and fulfill all of your needs, or it's just a temporary arrangement until you find something better.

Most of us have seen plenty of marriages that we would do anything to avoid duplicating, but how many of us have seen a marriage *in real life* worth learning more about? While growing up, I saw three very different marriages modeled by my parents and both sets of grandparents. Each had vastly different outcomes, too.

THE BUSINESS ARRANGEMENT

My dad's parents had a very business-like marriage. Granny was a nurse and when she married my grandfather, he told her he would pay off her student loans and she could pay him back with no interest. By the time the grandchildren were born, Granddad worked in Arlington, Texas, Monday through Friday and Granny lived in Wichita Falls, Texas, where the two of them shared a mailbox.

He had his side of the house set at seventy-five degrees; her side was set at sixty-eight. A sliding pocket door kept their two worlds from colliding. They met at the table for a home-cooked meal a few times each weekend and sat on the pew beside each other for Sunday morning services, but outside of that, they lived separate lives.

Everything was fair, mechanical, and obligatory. They were married well over forty years until my grandfather's death at age eighty-four. Several years after he passed, I asked Granny why she married him. She said, "Because I knew he would be a good provider." She also thought he was loyal, hard-working, and logical. To me, those sounded like good reasons to be in business with someone, but not reasons to get married.

THE AVERAGE (AT BEST) MARRIAGE

What I saw of my parents' marriage seemed normal. They had four children in six years, which by all standards is challenging in itself. They were full-time pastors and also worked for my mom's parents on large, arena-sized conferences that were usually held once a month, all out of town.

I remember hearing loud talking from their bedroom from the occasional fight about money and even the repercussions of exposed infidelity. Even though it was scary to me as a child, I would say they had an "average" or "normal" marriage.

My mom had very low self-esteem. I remember thinking she behaved like a doormat. It hurts me to even write those words, but she literally let my dad and a few others walk all over her. At that time in my life, I could already tell that I was wired differently than my mom. I had a strong personality, was smart for my age, and was keenly aware of and sensitive to the emotional climate in our house, including when things were just "off." I remember sensing my dad was cheating on my mom years before my feelings were validated, but how was I ever supposed to bring that up?

My parents' relationship seemed cold. It lacked the ooey-gooey romantic stuff and the mutual caring for each other. I could tell my mom wanted my dad's approval, affection, and attention, but since she rarely got those, she turned to other things like food and shopping for comfort. It didn't seem like my dad needed those things from my mom.

I think my dad could sense her desperation, which caused him to want less and less to do with her. When I asked my mom why she married my dad, she answered, "Because God told me to." That statement right there caused me to believe that if that's the kind of stuff God tells people to do, I would stay single. I truly thought to myself, *I can ruin my own life, thank you very much.*

In 2000, my parents' marriage of twenty-five years ended in divorce. On paper, the reasons were obvious and made sense, but even if there had been no infidelity or sexual orientation issue, I'm not sure their marriage would have lasted or been worth preserving anyway.

I was twenty-three and well aware of what was going on. My three sisters and I had front-row seats, watching our mom try to figure out who she was outside of being our dad's wife. Of course, she was a mom, too, but her identity had been completely wrapped up in being his wife. That's another reason I never wanted to get married.

> DEEP LOVE GROWS WITH VULNERABILITY AND FLOURISHES WITH INTERDEPENDENCE.

I was determined that I would never be dependent upon a man. I would always make enough money to provide for myself. I would never put myself in a position where if I was abandoned, I would be lost. I would never allow anyone to treat me like a doormat. I would never be weak. I would not give anyone the power to hurt me the way I saw my mom hurt. While these statements seemed like good ideas, they really were the recipe for being alone.

Love requires risk and trust. Deep love grows with vulnerability and flourishes with interdependence.

THE FOREVER-HONEYMOONERS MARRIAGE

On the other end of the spectrum were my mom's parents. They met later in their early fifties. Both had been married before. Poppa was a widower; Grandma was a widow and divorcee. My grandmother's first husband, whom she loved very much, died from an aneurysm a few years after they had a son (my uncle). Her second husband, my mom's father, turned out to be a violent man who tried to kill Grandma when she was pregnant with my mom. Needless to say, Grandma fled the situation and was a single mom of two children for nearly sixteen years.

One of the first things Poppa did after marrying Grandma was adopt my mom. My uncle was already an adult and on his own at the time. Outside of God and before I met Ted, Poppa was probably the best thing that ever happened to my family. He loved Grandma with his whole heart and was the best father to my mom. My grandparents' marriage was one I had the privilege of witnessing and using as a standard for what I wanted if I ever wed.

Every morning when they woke up, they would look at each other, complete with bed-head, no make-up, morning breath, and all, and Poppa would say, "There's the most beautiful woman I've ever seen." Then he would help Grandma put in her contact lenses and she would say, "There's the most handsome man I've ever seen." And this happened *every* morning.

As a child, I would witness this exchange and think to myself, *They are both a little whack-a-doodle. Don't they see all the wrinkles and brown spots? How can he think she is beautiful when her hair is crazy? How can she think he is handsome when he has hair coming out of his nose and ears?*

As I got older, it dawned on me that they didn't see any of that. They saw exactly what they wanted to in each other. They saw the love, the concern, the collection of memories of things they have been through together, the rescuing, the life partnership, the ministry, and so much more. They saw each other's hearts, and they truly were the most beautiful wife and handsomest husband.

They never argued. As an adult, I rationalized that away by saying it was because they never had to raise kids together. But even before Ted and I had children, we had a decent argument or two, so I decided that couldn't be it. Then I realized that they got married to love each other, to be together as much as possible, and to improve each other. That, my friends, made for a worthwhile marriage.

Ted

SERIAL WEDDINGS WITH SAD ENDINGS

I like to call myself a recovering introvert. As a deeply intro-verted child, I noticed more things because I wasn't talking or trying to draw attention to myself. When I was a kid, my family would have get-togethers often. It seemed like every holiday, my dad and his five sisters would all crash at somebody's house. Just imagine ten adults and sixteen children descending on a home and all of the different conversations that would take place. I loved it.

As we got older, these get-togethers became less frequent. Everyone got busy with their own lives, but often, there would be disagreements or misunderstandings that would alienate one or more of the sisters from the family. Most of the time, no one else had any idea why so-and-so was fighting with so-and-so, but I noticed. I saw how they looked at each other and spotted what they did when they thought the other one wasn't looking. I noted the distance that was being created.

My family is not the best example of reconciliation. However, I observed that all of my aunts chose men who were crazy about them. My dad, on the other hand, had three sour marriages. One was just young and dumb; the other two were cheating wives. He was crazy about them and they knew it. As a kid, I would say, "I'm never getting married" because of my father's experiences.

After my parents' divorce and my mom permanently leaving town, my dad felt he couldn't raise two boys on his own. So, he found wife number two. His second marriage started when I was six and ended when I was twenty-three. My aunts strongly disliked wife number two and I'm not sure they even attempted to hide it. They played nice because they wanted my dad to be around, but they soon found out that if she didn't want to be around, she'd suddenly say she didn't feel well and we all had to go home.

My dad was loyal to a fault and a martyr for keeping the peace rather than going head-to-head on issues and dealing with them. The way my dad handled his role as husband was through passivity. He would just let things go…let everything go, including affairs, demeaning comments, rebellious kids, arguing sisters—all of it. He just buried his head with a "they'll sort it out" mentality. He would never engage in an argument, which often wasn't what the situation needed. Some things are worth fighting for, worth standing up for, and worth calling people on the carpet so they can grow through the problems, not simply avoid them.

One of the issues Charity brought to my attention was that passivity can be just as devastating as aggression. It says, "I don't care," which likely led to many of the problems my dad experienced with his marriages. Even the Bible shares the importance of loving someone enough to bring correction. Charity told me she felt there was a better chance that something I *didn't* do would make her upset rather than something I did. She called them "sins of omission." She could see that bend toward passivity in me and wanted to be sure that I would engage and stand up toe-to-toe with her on issues.

FOCUS ON WHERE YOU WANT TO GO

It is essential to honestly assess what you've picked up from the marriages you've experienced and witnessed, both good and bad. Be open to the observations of your spouse as well. The point here is to grow and denial isn't the fastest route. When a growing point is made known, rather than refute it and become defensive, take a minute or two to process and ask yourself, *Could this be possible?* Since many habits, ideas, and beliefs are caught not taught, it's normal to pick up behaviors and patterns that are less than ideal.

There were many things I told myself I would never do because I saw them ultimately lead to my parents' divorce. What I have come to realize is the more you focus on what you're not going to do, the more you may actually wind up doing it.

> SINCE MANY HABITS, IDEAS, AND BELIEFS ARE CAUGHT NOT TAUGHT, IT'S NORMAL TO PICK UP BEHAVIORS AND PATTERNS THAT ARE LESS THAN IDEAL.

Have you ever noticed that when you're driving, if you look off to the side, the car starts to head in the direction you're looking? So many of us say things like:

+ "I'm never going to cheat like my dad did."
+ "I'm never going to lie like my mom did."
+ "I'm never going to berate my husband the way my mom did."
+ "I'm not going to be an addict like my dad."
+ "I won't let my husband walk all over me the way dad did to mom."

Then we are shocked when we realize we have followed some of their exact steps.

If what you're *not* going to do takes up too much of your focus, it is easy to head right toward it. Maybe not in the exact same manner as what you're trying to avoid, but the same root issue. Even though we think that negative attention will help us avoid something, it is *still* attention and takes up space in our minds and hearts. This approach is actually rooted in fear. If you pay close attention, the statements are more like:

+ "I hope I never hurt someone I love the way _____ did."
+ "Please don't let me become an addict just like _____."

◆ "What if I ruin a whole family because I can't keep my act together like _____?"

Pour all of your energy into becoming who you want to be rather than avoiding who you don't. Stop thinking about potential problems, redirect yourself toward the solution, and intentionally point your life and your marriage in the direction you want to go. Keep your focus on what you will do for yourself, your spouse, and your marriage and watch those things flourish.

HAPPY COUPLES

You may have heard the saying, "Show me your friends and I will show you your future." This concept can be found in the Bible. Proverbs 13:20 cautions, "*Walk with the wise and become wise; associate with fools and get in trouble*" (NLT). Paul tells us, "*Bad company corrupts good character*" (1 Corinthians 15:33). In other words, it's impossible to live the right life when you have the wrong friends, so choose wisely. Standards of what is acceptable and what isn't are best upheld when you hang out with like-minded people.

> POUR ALL OF YOUR ENERGY INTO BECOMING WHO YOU WANT TO BE RATHER THAN AVOIDING WHO YOU DON'T.

Ted and I are very conscious of how various couples make us feel about marriage and love in general. We don't spend time around couples who don't speak highly of each other or don't honor each other. Not having this moral code can be cancerous to strong relationships. Its effects go undetected for a while until one day you notice how sick, weak, and near death the relationship is. If you are surrounded by weak relationships, you will have no one you can reach out to in a time of crisis.

As a couple, you need to decide and commit to limiting your circle of close friends to those people who have marriages that inspire you and reflect who you want to be and how you want to live. Here are some of the criteria that we look for in friends:

+ Overall happy people
+ Speak highly of each other
+ Affectionate in a healthy way
+ Speak of marriage as a lifelong and worthy commitment
+ Honest and able to discuss real-life issues
+ Humble and real
+ Fun to be with

I'm sure our friends have additional positive attributes, but my point is that couples like this are a joy to be around and truly energize us. With these types of friends, you can glean strength in areas you feel weak before it becomes a sinking-ship situation. Good friends will notice when things are off and ask questions to help you find solutions. Allowing yourself to be seen in your own weakness will help your marriage find solid ground even in the hardest times.

LISTEN AND LEARN

I love to see older couples holding hands, shopping together, vacationing, and even sitting on the same side in a restaurant booth. That tells the story of enduring love. If given the chance, I enjoy asking them their secrets to a happy marriage and the responses range from super sweet to laughing-so-hard-you-cry funny. Sadly, our culture doesn't demonstrate an honor toward older, long-married couples. They are treated as though they are irrelevant. Yet there is so much we can learn from them. Spend time around couples who have been married a long time and are still happy.

Before Ted and I had children, we hadn't really ever seen a marriage with kids that looked like anything we wanted. Everyone seemed to be frazzled as they carted their kids from one activity to the next while eating fast food in the car. The relationships felt like tactical check-ins of who had which kid. "What's for dinner?" sounded like a curse.

We wanted kids but were slightly terrified of what that would do to our marriage. Thankfully, we found an amazing couple at church and were able to observe what life looked like in their home. They were perfectly imperfect, full of love and grace toward each other, raising four biological sons and an adopted daughter.

Everything that came at them was handled as a team. They both served their family with everything they had and honored each other for what they contributed. They kissed, hugged, and smiled at each other, which was inspiring and heart-warming. We have had the privilege of calling them friends for nearly two decades now and are continually inspired by their marriage.

I am honestly not sure when Ted and I would have pulled the trigger on having kids if we hadn't met them. I don't know how long the fear of kids changing us would have lasted. Simply listening and learning from those ahead of us encouraged us to get on the roller coaster of parenting and truly enjoy the ride.

It's been a blessing to be able to ask them questions about raising our four wildly different children. I'm the type of person who doesn't like learning from my own mistakes. I would rather learn from someone else's and avoid the pain altogether. If you don't have a couple who immediately come to mind that you could learn from, ask God to bring them into your life.

One time, we were at our church's Valentine's Dinner and they asked around to find the couple who had been married the longest. The particular couple they found that night had been married over fifty years. When asked what their secret was, the husband said, "We have four kids and we always said whoever asked for the divorce had to take the kids." Everyone burst out laughing at that humorous comment, especially those who knew what it takes to raise four children.

I'm personally a big fan of finding inspiration from long-wed couples who obviously still love each other. You can find them in your church, your neighborhood, at the grocery store, or at the gym. When you do find such a couple, ask them to share their insights about marriage.

FIND INSPIRATION FROM LONG-WED COUPLES WHO OBVIOUSLY STILL LOVE EACH OTHER.

You could discover how much fun they were still having after all of those years and undoubtedly all of the ups and downs they contained. One of my favorite things about spending time around couples who have made it through a life's worth of experiences is seeing the joy and appreciation they hold for each other.

Another adorable couple we know who have been married nearly fifty years have some funny sayings. When she asks him how he's doing, he says, "Well, I woke up on the right side of the ground." I hope with everything within me that we have that kind of joy and humor when we reach their age. I never get tired of making Ted laugh so hard he cries. Being around other couples who still enjoy making their spouses laugh as well is the best.

One of our most dear happy-couple friends are like an extra set of parents to us. They were both widowed by spouses they loved dearly and bravely chose to give love another go. They take such good care of each other and laugh together regularly. They are generous, friendly, and loyal to each other and their friends.

They give me hope that if anything untimely were to happen to me or Ted, the other could find love again. I cannot imagine the strength it took to make it through the loss of the love of a lifetime, but I am thankful they let us ask them questions about how they do life now as a couple and what space their first spouses have in their lives.

> *The beginning of wisdom is this: Get wisdom. Though it cost all you have, get understanding.* (Proverbs 4:7)

Another translation of this verse puts it this way: "*Getting wisdom is the wisest thing you can do! And whatever else you do, develop good judgment*" (NLT).

Humble yourself to learn from someone ahead of you. They don't have to be ages older than you, just ahead. Spend time digging for their pearls of wisdom that often hide in everyday conversation and observation. Be willing to implement what you learn. At some point, you may become someone else's role model.

STAY CONNECTED TO GOD

We can definitely attest to the fact that our marriage is better because of our individual relationships with God and our joint relationship with God. There were times when events or circumstances seemed so out of our control that prayer was the only option. While our marriage has been amazing, we weren't always sure it was going to go as we planned. When one of us was acting like a fool, the other had to stand on faith and believe for our marriage. When one of us was sick or weak, the other would cover in prayer and be strong.

The Bible talks about marriage in such a profound way. I'll admit, I sometimes got derailed at the idea of "submission" (see Ephesians 5:21–33) but if you read the passages in context, it's easy if the husband is truly loving as Christ loves the church. When you stay connected to God and His Word, it keeps your posture in check. How you speak to your spouse, how you view him or her in your mind, and your level of marriage as service hinge upon this posture. Meditating on how God designed marriage helps to preserve it.

PRAYING TOGETHER AS A COUPLE WILL UNITE YOUR HEARTS AND REFOCUS YOUR VISION.

There were times when only God could change a situation in our lives. Staying connected to Him gave us the confidence to ask for the change. When we neglected this relationship, we felt embarrassed to even ask...and then suffered for it. God will also help you see what is really significant when there is struggle or strife. Our culture wants us to take offense as our first response, but God's design is for us to love first. Keeping God's plan and heart for you in mind will help you diffuse rash emotion and respond in a way that brings healing and peace.

Praying together as a couple will unite your hearts and refocus your vision. When Ted prays for me and our family, my heart swells with love and fills with a sense of safety and protection. I love that Ted covers us and defends us from not only potential physical threats but spiritual ones as well. He prays with such humility and sincerity that any grudges I might have had simply wash away.

Your prayers don't have to be elaborate, contrived, or long. Sometimes, I will just reach over and put my hand on Ted's arm while we're driving around and say a simple one-sentence prayer. It can be something like, "Lord, help us work hard on the right things and leave the results up to You." When your spirit is connected to God, your marriage will reap the benefits of love, joy, peace, patience, kindness, goodness, and faithfulness. (See Galatians 5:22.)

Making your connection to God a priority helps to keep your marriage a priority. Marriage was designed to be a testimony and a reflection of His love for us. We know how much our marriage means to us, our children, and anyone who sees Ted and me together.

May God be glorified in all of our marriages as we stay connected to Him.

10

Commitment

Commitment is the foundation of any quality relationship. When you near graduation from high school and go to visit colleges, they often ask for a commitment letter to ensure you actually attend that college. Otherwise, they'd give your spot to someone else.

As a nurse, I had to sign a contract when I accepted my first hospital position. I acknowledged I was going to fulfill my part of the agreement for all of the training and investment they were making in me.

Marriage is first and foremost a commitment to our spouse. The vows and promises we make speak to the level of commitment required throughout a lifetime. We agree to love them "for better, for worse, for richer, for poorer, in sickness and in health."

> YOUR MARRIAGE WILL HAVE BOTH BETTER DAYS AND WORSE DAYS, BUT THAT SHOULDN'T AFFECT THE LEVEL OF YOUR COMMITMENT.

It's interesting how these standard vows position us to protect, endure, and fulfill our commitment. The first vow is usually "for better or for worse." We should take more than a moment at the altar to reflect on this core of commitment. As two extremes, they could not be further apart. "For better" can seem impossible on your wedding day. How does it get better than the most important day of the rest of your life? But remember, the honeymoon occurs after the wedding, which might be a little stressful if everything didn't go according to plan. "For worse" seems easier to imagine if you have even the slightest degree of pessimism or skepticism in your personality.

Your marriage will have both better days and worse days, but that shouldn't affect the level of your commitment. One of the reasons Charity and I have such a strong marriage is that we celebrate during the better days and we draw closer to each other during the worse ones. Sometimes, these better/worse days are circumstances that come at us from life and outside forces, but other times, they are internal situations either one or both of us created. Commitment for better or worse covers both. Loving another person and being committed to them includes the times when they are less than stellar and vice versa.

Charity

BETTER DAYS VS. WORSE DAYS

CHILDREN

The days we received our gifts of children would qualify as better days for sure. We have had four of these very exciting days that were all different but wonderful memories. They are our four arrows we hope to launch into the world at their appointed times. At their births, we were filled with gratitude and overwhelming love for these new little lives. Looking in their eyes and seeing the promise of a future made all the pain worth it.

Each child came with a struggle and, at the same time, many blessings and miracles.

When you commit to each other in marriage and bring kids into the world, you commit to standing by each other during the better or worse days of parenting, too. Before we pulled the goalie and tried to get pregnant, Ted and I went back and forth several times on whether we were ready. I personally struggled with a fear of infertility. Growing up, I had some complications from ovarian cysts and irregular cycles. I felt pessimistic about my chances of becoming a mother. And I was terrified by the idea of not being able to give Ted children and what that might do to our relationship.

To our surprise, our firstborn was a one-trick wonder. We conceived so quickly that it made me nervous about getting pregnant

> WHEN YOU COMMIT TO EACH OTHER AND BRING KIDS INTO THE WORLD, YOU STAND BY EACH OTHER DURING THE BETTER OR WORSE DAYS OF PARENTING, TOO.

too soon after he was born. It had been a long time since either of us had been around babies, yet when Luke arrived, I was able to feel Ted's commitment to me in a deeper way. I didn't want more than one child if the majority of the responsibility fell on me, but that wasn't the case at all, which made me happy to have three more. Ted changed every diaper when he was home from work and not only cared for our newborn son, he cared for me, too.

We both remained committed to our fundamental belief that our relationship came first and being parents came second. Our marriage will always get our best. Seeing this commitment fleshed out made the love I felt for Ted grow exponentially. We were committed as a couple and as parenting partners.

A little over a year later, Ted and I started to talk about having another baby. Since we were enjoying Luke so much, we pretty much leapt into the process right away. After such a fast conception with Luke, we assumed it would happen again quickly. Month one, no luck. Month two, nothing. Month three, four, five, six, seven, eight, nine, ten, eleven—nada, nope, not happening.

By month six, I was feeling distraught. The same fear of infertility welled up within me. I was crying regularly, which put more work on Ted. Commitment during this time was everything. I would question Ted's love and he was there every time, reminding me we were in this together and I was enough for him.

After a long year and tons of prayer, there were two pink lines on the home pregnancy test. Baby Kate was on her way. She brought so much joy and was a bundle of sunshine. We were so distracted by her, Luke, and the joys of life that baby Natalie decided to join the party seventeen short months later. Three kids meant Ted and I were outnumbered. Ted's schooling started when Natalie was eight months old. We had three children ages five and under, so it was chaos central.

TIME FOR BABY NO. 4

A couple of years later, both Ted and I wanted another child. Since I was nearing thirty-five, we wanted to get that party started and over before the beloved ovaries started to wear out. We decided to go for it and conceived within a few months. The whole family came into town a month later so we told them all the good news. We were elated to find out that one of my sisters was due at the same time. On top of that, one of my good friends was also expecting. It was exciting.

I was set to deliver two months before my thirty-fifth birthday. Perfect! All worked out according to my plans...or so I thought. I began to experience odd symptoms. For instance, I would feel unbearably cold, opposite of my pregnant norm, which included daily servings of crushed ice, tank tops, and flip flops, even in winter. I told Ted something wasn't right, yet he reassured me that all was fine and I shouldn't worry.

We went to the doctor just before the holidays and saw a very tiny embryo with a low heart rate of around a hundred beats per minute. I also had low progesterone levels and was immediately given a prescription to raise them. Having never had issues like this before with my other three pregnancies, our doctor was concerned and scheduled us for a follow-up ultrasound after the New Year. Ted was prepared for better; I was prepared for worse.

When we went in for our follow-up appointment, the technician took us to the "special hallway" separate from the normal ultrasound rooms. As the ultrasound began, I immediately saw that my intuition was right. Our sweet little baby had no heartbeat. I wept while Ted froze in disbelief. He was in his obstetrics clinical rotations by this time and went very medical trying to figure out what happened.

FOR WORSE...

This was definitely one of our "for worse" days. Our commitment through that day, and the other days of grief and sorrow that followed, caused us to grow together rather than apart. Without full knowledge of what was going to happen, we decided to allow nature to take its course and let my body to do the work of miscarrying. It took seventeen longs days of waiting for that to begin.

I was in the middle of working on a client's hair when I doubled over in pain. I had only been told to expect something like a bad period.

I thought I was dying.

I called a close friend, who came over to watch the kids as Ted cared for me in our bathroom. He began timing what we soon realized were contractions and talked with the doctor-on-call to learn what we needed to do.

Then we were told that everything I was experiencing was "normal" and it was going to last a few more hours. I could have punched a wall, I was so mad at our obstetrician for not telling us this was what we should expect. The next day, we had an early morning appointment to make sure all was clear to rule out the need for surgery. Thankfully, it was.

A couple of days later, it was time for church. Nope. I told Ted I didn't want to go. I was mad at God and knew I would cry through the whole service. In his loving way, Ted told me it was okay to cry at church and my heart needed to grieve. He told me God could handle my feelings and He was there to comfort me. Skipping church could begin to separate me from God, Ted cautioned me. "What would stop you from not going the next time or the next? When would you really be ready to go back?" I couldn't argue with his logic. I needed to push through my reluctance of facing the pain of the loss and just let it wash over me.

So, we went and sat in the back. Ted held my hand and got tissues for me throughout the service. He was right. I did need to be there even though I fought it. Through worship, the walls of anger and sadness began to come down and I could just be sad about what happened rather than feeling singled out for this tragedy.

The next several days and weeks consisted of moments when I was fine and moments when I would think about what could have been. I was concerned that I might never stop crying. I shared this sincere fear with Ted and his answer to me literally gave me such freedom that I believe it curtailed much of the duration of my grief. He said, "I don't want you to worry about when you are going to stop crying. It's okay to cry. You can cry every day if you need to. I am here for you and we will get through this."

I had never been granted such permission to cry. I felt like long-term crying equaled depression and I didn't want to be depressed or unable to care for my family. I also knew I didn't want to camp out at this loss and never move on. This wasn't going to be how our story ended. I told Ted to watch and make sure I didn't go into a dark or deep depression while I let myself feel and grieve. I knew he would pay attention and intervene if necessary. Thankfully, we were able to heal and move on.

A 10TH ANNIVERSARY PRESENT

Our tenth anniversary was a little over three months later. We celebrated by taking our first legit vacation to Riviera Maya, Mexico. It was a great respite following our loss, on top of the stress of nursing school and homeschooling. We celebrated all that our ten years contained and what we made it through. Between the beach, romantic meals, and everything else our all-inclusive resort provided, we came home with the best souvenir ever: our fourth child, Presley.

She has a testimony all her own as well. Knowing she was our last child, I was determined to enjoy the pregnancy. At our twenty-week appointment, we brought all three kids to find out the baby's gender and let them observe the ultrasound process. I immediately saw it was a girl, but then noticed the medical staff was spending a lot of time looking at her brain, spine, and umbilical cord. Being that I was going to be thirty-six when she was born, the fear of genetic issues crept in. All of my files said, "Advanced maternal age," as if my uterus had one foot in the grave.

I asked the technician if she could explain the lengthy scan and she said we would be consulting with a genetics specialist. It felt like the room was spinning. I wasn't prepared for this. Our kids were there, so I couldn't take the time to thoroughly process the information. I had to be strong for them.

The doctor told us that our baby had cysts on her brain and a single-artery umbilical cord. These issues didn't wave many flags on their own, but together, they indicated a possible chromosomal issue.

I thank God we had a Christian obstetrician, Dr. Richard Presley, who not only prayed with us, but also offered ultrasounds whenever I wanted them to ease my mind so I could sleep at night. He told us he felt very good about our chances of having a healthy baby and he would do whatever he could to help us feel that way, too. Any time my mind would wander to the "worse" of what could happen, Ted would bring my focus back to enjoying the pregnancy. He knows I like factual details, so he reminded me that stress would not help the baby. Since I couldn't do anything else to change our situation, the one thing I *could* do was not stress out.

A few months later, Presley was born totally healthy, with no growth restrictions. Her birth was one of our "better" days. She is a daily reminder of Ted's commitment to me. We had already picked out her name; having a Dr. Presley was a happy coincidence. He sang "Happy Birthday" when she was being delivered and I believe he was a gift from God to me at that time in my life.

Perhaps your marriage has gone through loss. Statistics point to death, major illnesses, special needs children, and other hardships as things that stack the deck against marriages. While we have not experienced all of these issues, we have dealt with the pressure and pain from a few of them. It's not easy.

Sometimes, our minds trick us into thinking that it would be easier to deal with life's problems if we were apart, but that's not what the commitment of marriage is about. It's about partnering through the pain, not giving up when you're tired, not trying to go it alone or avoiding counseling or help, and definitely not leaving God out. The "worse" days are the proving ground of the commitment. They are the times when love reaches new depths. Don't rob your marriage of this valuable gift. Don't waiver in your commitment. Talk openly if you're struggling.

If all we experienced were "better" days, we may never have known the true depth of our commitment. In fact, our love grew more during the worse days than the better ones. When you experience your worse days, your spouse needs to be able to look into your eyes and know you are going to fight with them, not against them. This is huge! It's easy to take anger, grief, or disappointment out on our spouse, to make them feel the brunt of our pain, rather than be the one who bears it with us and shares the burden.

Your spouse is going to draw from deep within to comfort and embrace you, not judge you or push you away. When you go through those worse days, remember your wedding vows and promises. Say them aloud if it helps you. Remember, you promised to love, honor, and cherish your spouse for better or worse, in sickness and in health, for richer or poorer.

Charity

COMMITMENT TO EACH OTHER'S GROWTH

Our investment in each other has brought an abundant return in personal growth, which has been a priority for us. We want to grow both as a couple and as individuals. I have always had a life coach personality even before it became popular. I enjoy helping people figure out what their next steps are and how to manifest them. I was ecstatic to go through the "what do I want to be when I grow up?" discovery process with Ted as he searched for a fulfilling career.

When he landed on nursing, I knew we were committing to a long-haul journey with a steep cost. A few years prior, he supported me through cosmetology school, so I was ready to return the favor. After all, he was miserable at his warehouse job. We were both willing to take drastic measures for him to have some joy and satisfaction at work.

Earning his nursing degree was a four-and-a-half-year undertaking that put an immense amount of pressure on both of us. It would have been impossible had we both not been committed to the outcome. Ted felt the pressure of keeping up his grades and maintaining his part-time job so we could have health insurance. I felt the pressure of carrying the majority of household, childcare, and earning responsibilities. There were plenty of worse days that could have worn away at our relationship. But commitment held us together.

Marriage is a long-term investment. The returns are cumulative and rich. Both of you must give 100 percent to experience maximum benefits. One-sided commitments create resentment and crack the foundation. It's normal to experience temptation and some degree of internal questioning, *Can I do this?* How you handle these thoughts can strengthen or weaken your marriage.

If you ever feel you are near a breaking point, be honest with your spouse. Let them know, "Right now, I need you more than ever." Go to them with your weakness and ask for help. Don't hide in shame and tempt fate further. Commitment for better or worse isn't always glamorous or wrinkle-free. It is often a collage of brutal and beautiful moments you have experienced together.

Love that has exercised and experienced commitment grows stronger. It is a testimony to your children, family, and everyone who knows you. Love believes the best and is willing to work through things rather than abandon the challenge. With our cultural climate encouraging us to bail at the first offense, we need to remain committed to each other. Love endures. It clings to the hope of better days to come and supports our spouse in times when they need it. It's willing to receive that same support when we are the weak one.

> COMMITMENT IS OFTEN A COLLAGE OF BRUTAL AND BEAUTIFUL MOMENTS YOU HAVE EXPERIENCED TOGETHER.

IN SICKNESS AND IN HEALTH

SICKNESS

Commitment through sickness is one of the most challenging issues a marriage can face. When one of you has acute or chronic pain, mental illness, disease, addiction, or an injury, it shifts a good portion of life's load on to the other partner. The longer the duration, the deeper the commitment must go.

We have had the privilege of witnessing some strong married couples battle cancer, strokes, depression, addiction, car accidents, and more while remaining firmly side by side. We have also seen such issues tear marriages apart.

If you are the supporting spouse, it is imperative that you allow people to support you as well. Please don't let your pride make you think you should do it all on your own. Sure, there are days when the burden is bearable. But before it becomes too much, reach out for help. Whether it's letting friends help with a meal or hiring a housekeeper, do what it takes to stay sane and healthy yourself. If you have children and they are old enough, delegate appropriate responsibilities to them.

This is one of the biggest reasons it is necessary to be part of a community. It is hard to shoulder this alone. A good community strengthens your marriage.

HELPING OTHERS

If you know a couple who are struggling with tough issues, be the hands and feet of Jesus and offer help to them. I don't mean, "Call me if you need anything," because they will never call. Be specific about how you can help; if you can, set a date and time to do it. Be practical. Mow the lawn, do the laundry, babysit the kids, take a meal to them, go to the store, or even offer coffee and a listening ear. Many hands make the burden light. Feeling the love, care, and concern of a friend is energizing and relieving.

I ask God to help me anticipate someone's needs. I am not always the best gift-giver, but I *am* the queen of practicality. You know what parts of life can be done by someone else. What a gift to help support another marriage! These are some of the best seeds your marriage can sow.

HEALTH: THE FINAL FRONTIER

Our current joint venture is getting and *staying* in better health. Over the course of our marriage, we have seen that we both need discipline when it comes to diet and nutrition. We have struggled with weight for most of our lives—on opposite ends of the spectrum. This has made meal-planning a challenge. At first, whenever I would try to lose weight, I would watch in frustration as Ted ate whatever he wanted while I gingerly dipped my fork in dressing before stabbing it into my not-so-sexy salad. Of course, this was while Ted was in his late twenties and early thirties. Things were about to catch up for him. Bwahahaha!

A few years and children later, Ted was sporting the tiny dad-belly and I was still up all of the pregnancy pounds with no idea how to juggle everything. We found another nutritional plan that showed promise; a couple of months in, Ted was under his goal weight, with sagging pants, and I plateaued at seven pounds down. The only thing sagging was my ego.

After baby number four, the weight gain, the stress of Ted's schooling, and bulging spinal discs and sacroiliac issues in my back caused me to look into the scary idea of weight loss surgery. I had a medical consultation, only to learn I wasn't "sick enough" to qualify. I *could* qualify if I stayed at that weight for two more years—but what a punishment to myself!

During these years, Ted was more or less taking his cues from me. He supported whatever I wanted or needed to feel better. He never put pressure on me; he just wanted me to feel good about myself. In the meantime, Ted was diagnosed with sleep apnea unrelated to his weight, but they said weight loss would help.

I took another stab at trying to lose weight on my own, but again relapsed into old habits. Our move to Houston was coming up, so I decided this was my chance for the fresh start I needed to be healthy. I was going to eat right, work out every day, and be a whole new healthy me. Look out, world!

I did really well the first three days. Then the excitement wore off and I began eating for comfort, stress relief, ease, relieving loneliness, fear...but never eating to nourish or really care for myself. I had let myself down again and it felt like I let *everyone* down. I no longer believed myself when I said I would stick to something.

Almost two years later, I reached a breaking point. Thankfully, Ted was by my side and ready to be healthy with me. A friend called; she cared enough to talk to me about my health and help me get started. One. More. Time. I was cautiously optimistic and white-knuckling, but humble enough to take each scared step.

> HEALTH IS AN ACT OF LOVE TO YOUR SPOUSE THAT SAYS, "I WANT TO DO MY BEST TO BE AROUND FOR YOU AS LONG AS I CAN."

The success of this lifestyle change was two-fold. First, because we decided to do it together, Ted and I found something that worked for both of us. It included a dietary balance that enabled us to stay in it long-term. Second, I took to heart the idea that I can only love Ted from the love I give myself.

I am a better wife because I have chosen health. Ted is a better husband because he has chosen health. I write these words out of full awareness that this is a daily choice and I admit it is still a difficult one. Together, we are disciplining ourselves for the ultimate freedom health brings. After many years of doing it wrong, we are finally on a path that is producing progress and I can tangibly feel the honor that choosing health gives our marriage.

Health has many benefits in life—in the bedroom, chasing kids, building dreams, and having fun. It's an act of love to your spouse that says, "I want to do my best to be around for you as long as I can. I don't want to be a burden to you so I will do everything in my power to pursue health."

The love that it takes to say, "I know you, I can see everything that's going on, and I am right here with you" is exponentially larger and richer than the love it takes to simply say, "I do." This type of love says, "I'm *staying I do*" and lives the vow of "in sickness and health."

COMMON CENTS

Besides time, money is another area where we are able to show our commitment to each other as a couple. We talk more in depth about money in chapter seven. Now, we are looking at the commitment aspect of "for richer, for poorer."

There are numerous contributing factors to bank balance fluctuations, from spending behavior to medical issues. Some factors are out of our control. The most concrete way to demonstrate commitment in the area of finances is to agree on where the money will go, for what purposes, and stick with it. Be on the same page and let your fierce loyalty shine here.

A shortage of money by itself doesn't usually take down a marriage. It's usually the behavior it reveals and represents that scrapes away at the protective trust layer. Here are a couple of examples we have witnessed personally:

+ A couple with two small children are in financially challenging times. Their marriage is feeling the pressure. The wife is in full-blown fear/panic mode as they have had to move in with her mother to survive. In the middle of this crisis, the husband secretly goes off skiing with his buddies and charges the trip to their credit card. Between that and other character issues, the marriage ends in divorce.

+ A couple who are living paycheck to paycheck have stable jobs, but don't make a ton of money. The end of the month is always a challenge, but the wife will not neglect her elaborate nails or hair appointments for anything. Instead of paying the electric and water bills with the money designated for them for two or three months, she gets her nails and hair done. Since she takes care of the bills, her husband is unaware of the misappropriation of funds until both their water and electricity are shut off. Another marriage ends in divorce.

In these two specific examples, money may have been tight and the financial situation stressful, but that wasn't what caused the marriages to collapse. The selfish approaches and destructive behaviors are to blame.

WHEN IT'S OUT OF YOUR CONTROL

One of the things I love about our marriage is that I know Ted and I will both do whatever it takes, whenever it's required. We are fully committed to work harder and cut back when necessary. This doesn't mean I don't get scared; it just means I don't feel alone during hard times. Ted doesn't get so worked up about financial things like I do because he's lived through much simpler times than I have. I lean on his stability and am grateful for it.

There are times when bills crop up that are out of our control. We may have an aging parent who has worsening medical issues, a child who needs tutoring, or some other challenge. Sometimes, we must spend money to take care of a situation we didn't anticipate.

Commitment and unity are two of the best gifts you can give each other during these seasons, whether they are short or long-term. Commit to open communication. Commit to fighting these times together, side by side, rather than fighting each other. Commit to your plan of what bills get paid first and stick with it. Commit to keeping the words that come out of your mouth positive. Commit to hold and comfort each other when fear or concern grips you. And commit to doing the best you both can at reducing the financial burden.

11

Chasing Dreams

Ted

FRESH-START DREAMS

One of the most exciting things to do for your marriage is to chase dreams together. Dream-chasing can be simple or complex, depending on the size of the dream and effort needed to make it a reality. When Charity and I first met, she was already planning to move from Dallas, Texas, to Nashville, Tennessee, and I decided to go with her.

This move fulfilled the dream of a fresh start for us as individuals and as a couple. The Dallas/Fort Worth area held so many memories of the stupid stuff we had done. Just driving around our old stomping grounds caused flashbacks of things we weren't proud of and times that caused us pain.

Outside of Charity's college years in Tulsa, Oklahoma, and a brief stay in Virginia for me, neither of us had lived anywhere outside of DFW.

> IN MARRIAGE, HAVING BOTH PARTIES FOCUSED ON THE SAME DREAM INVITES CREATIVITY, RESOURCEFULNESS, AND THE EXPONENTIAL REWARD OF TEAMWORK AND UNITY.

We wanted a new adventure with new memories made together. We called this our "leave and cleave" season. This cross-country move taught us a lot about each other and strengthened our bond. We found out rather quickly how strong we were together and how we could depend on each other. It forced us to create new habits, friendships, and routines that included each other. Despite the growing pains, it was pretty awesome and I'm glad we took the leap. In marriage, having both parties focused on the same dream invites creativity, resourcefulness, and the exponential reward of teamwork and unity.

EVOLVING CAREER DREAMS

There is no feeling quite like investing in your spouse and having them invested in you. This is an essential element of a thriving marriage. It is the lifeblood for increasing worth and confidence, which keeps your marriage fresh and engaging rather than stagnant.

Many marriages are stuck because the individuals are stuck. If no one's growing, no one's changing. Conversations are a drag, interest is waning, and you get bored hearing the same stories and complaints every day.

If you hear your spouse bemoaning their job and feeling miserable, it may be time to help them evolve. Help them dream. Be a sounding board so they can bounce ideas off of you.

Unless, of course, you want to keep hearing those same complaints every day.

One of Charity's business ventures was a talent agency for up-and-coming Christian bands. In her heart and mind, it was going to grow and become a sought-after company because she was a hard worker and put her all into it. While she saw marginal success, the business was only able to financially sustain her employees, not her. She took on a part-time job to pay herself because the agency couldn't.

> IF YOU HEAR YOUR SPOUSE BEMOANING THEIR JOB AND FEELING MISERABLE, IT MAY BE TIME TO HELP THEM EVOLVE.

After four years or so, this was very stressful and draining on her. I knew she couldn't stay under this stress much longer, so I encouraged her to consider trying something else. We agreed to let that business go so she could move on to something else that used more of her skills and fit her personality needs.

This transition was initially hard for her; she felt like she wasted four years of her life and earning potential. She wasn't used to things not working out the way she planned because she's a doer and a hard worker. But she learned a lot during those four years— it was almost as if she had earned a business degree.

Charity began to think about her options and what she actually wanted to do. She's so talented that there were almost too many options. Everyone wanted her to be a star in their multi-level marketing business, but sales had burned her out. She wanted to create a business where people came to her for a product or service, not one where she had to hard sell or cold call.

And Charity didn't want a *job*; she wanted to create a business. She wanted flexibility, higher income potential, more quality time with friends, and the ability to be creative all while working from home. Basically, a "unicorn"—that's her word for anything that is one-in-a-million or super-specific. With her high standards and attention to detail, she's a "unicorn hunter."

She shared a revelation with me: becoming a cosmetologist could check off all of her boxes. Within days of that conversation, she had researched and enrolled in cosmetology school. I know that if something passes her standards, then for sure it will pass mine. She always has our best interests at heart and hunts for the best deal with intensity.

Charity has a strong desire to always contribute financially to our family, so she was concerned about attending cosmetology school full-time. Combined with her responsibilities at home, she couldn't hold down a job, too, yet she didn't want all the pressure of providing to fall on me. Nor did she want our family to end up in a desperate situation.

One of the exciting things I discovered while putting Charity through school was that I could provide for our family on my own. More importantly, Charity realized that, too.

When we said "yes" to this dream, we didn't have all the details, but we had faith—faith in God and faith in each other that we would do whatever it took to complete the process. Chasing dreams together lets you reach for something even when you're not sure how it will work out.

MY CAREER DREAM

It did not take long for Charity's styling business to out-earn what I was making at the warehouse. Over the next seventeen months, we added two more children and her at-home set-up enabled her to both work and enjoy being a mom. Everything was going great...except my job was becoming less fulfilling and more frustrating. I was coming home a grump, with the same set of complaints nearly every day, and it was wearing on Charity.

This set of circumstances caused me to revisit the idea of going into nursing, which had been one of my biggest dreams. I've always visualized myself helping people, saving lives, bandaging wounds, and otherwise caring for others. However, I wasn't dreaming of nursing school or forty to sixty hours of reading and studying each week. I wasn't dreaming of stressful tests, demanding clinical practices, writing papers, or the never-ending possibility of failing a class and falling a semester or year behind. I wasn't dreaming of the stress it would put on my wife, our children, or myself.

CHASING DREAMS TOGETHER LETS YOU REACH FOR SOMETHING EVEN WHEN YOU'RE NOT SURE HOW IT WILL WORK OUT.

When you have a dream, you might see the end result, but not all the steps in between. For us, the first thing that came to Charity's mind was every single one of those steps. She anticipated the difficult journey long before I did. In fact, one of the most sobering discussions of our married life concerned the effects of a long-term college commitment on a marriage and family. I don't know the statistics but I do know plenty of marriages crumble under the pressure—and I know why. It was crazy hard. It squeezed all sides of our marriage, especially Charity's top need for quality time with me.

MIRACULOUS PROVISION

I've never been a worrier. If I feel something in my soul, I confidently and calmly put all of my energy into it. Just as I knew I would move up to Nashville and get a job in a warehouse, I knew I would become a nurse. I'm also keenly aware that it would have been impossible without Charity's love and dedicated support.

When I struggled to believe in myself, she was there, staring in my eyes and telling me I was going to do great. Friends, there is no freedom or power like someone believing in you. And I'm talking about someone who knows all of your weaknesses, flaws, and insecurities. When that person looks straight into your soul and says, "Your strengths are more than enough," it propels you to reach your goal and look forward to the next one.

When it came time to "do the dream" and apply for college, we quickly found that there weren't many scholarship opportunities for non-traditional aged students like me, at age thirty-six. Because Charity is the detailed one out of the two of us, she filled out all of my financial aid paperwork and sent it in. Almost instantly, God dropped it in Charity's spirit that all of my college expenses were going to be covered in full and I would graduate debt-free. This was huge considering how hard we worked early on to get out of debt. She didn't announce it to the whole world—"What if it didn't happen?"—but she had a strong sense it would come to pass.

I enrolled in my classes in faith while awaiting the response from financial aid. Originally, my warehouse employer said they would work with my college schedule and allow me to keep working to bring home some income and give our family health insurance. With Charity being self-employed, she couldn't provide insurance for our family. Right after I enrolled in classes, however, my employer decided they wouldn't work with my college schedule.

I could either drop out or quit my job. As you can imagine, Charity freaked out. She was livid and scared, with just cause. I was upset but knew in my heart that God had something better.

We decided that the warehouse job was a dead-end and therefore not an option, so I got a grocery job that offered benefits to part-time employees. Great! Then after going through the hiring process, I learned benefits for part-timers didn't kick in until after a year and a half or so.

Now what?

Within a week, my sister-in-law called and suggested I apply for a job at the bank where she worked because they offered health insurance for part-timers as well as other amazing benefits. For most, the hiring process with this company took four to six weeks, but because my sister-in-law had a local connection for me, I was interviewed and hired in less than a week. This job not only came with full insurance benefits after only thirty days, but also supplemental childcare and twelve weeks *paid* paternity leave. Who gives paternity leave, much less twelve weeks paid to the dad?! It was a miracle.

Then we received another blessing: the financial aid letter came and showed grants that covered everything at our local community college for the entire first year. We were both blown away. In Charity's mind, it was, "One year down, three and a half more to go."

Semester after semester was miraculously paid for and I received my bachelor's degree in nursing with honors completely debt-free. Charity jokingly says she should've received a partial degree since she helped me study and obtain the financial aid. She just can't handle blood, guts, or bodily fluids.

PLOT TWIST

One Sunday at church, the pastor asked, "What's next?" In Charity's mind, *our* next was what we were doing right then: my nursing career. She didn't expect that she was about to venture into new territory herself. This next step came out of nowhere because life was really good at that time. Her business was flourishing, she was teaching at church, we had a great community and friends, and I was about to graduate, so we would have two incomes once more. Charity had been so busy helping me reach my next goal and manage the family that she hadn't even considered her own personal and professional growth in a while. That particular church service didn't end with her having a plan or seeing a vision, but a space grew in her heart for *something*.

Just before my final semester, Charity and I spoke at a relationships conference in Houston. While we were there, without us knowing it, God was leading Charity into her next dream. Something felt right about being back in Texas, even though we both felt we'd never live there again. I guess that's what happens when you say "never." We were struggling to find a house that fit our super-sized family, plus my dad, in Nashville, so we were already on the hunt for something. We weren't able to find anything that met our needs and our budget so we literally felt stuck.

But at that conference, God laid it on our hearts to sow a big seed for direction on our housing situation. We had no idea how drastic that direction was going to be. Charity started to have feelings about where this new house was located.

Two days after we returned from Houston, we were talking in the parking lot of a home goods store (where all significant conversations occur) when Charity asked me how I would feel about moving to Houston. She foresaw two possibilities in her "next" phase: she could stay in Nashville and grow her influence on a slower, smaller scale, or accelerate it by moving to Houston. In less than a minute, we both agreed that despite how crazy this sounded, moving was the right thing to do. And with Charity's mom and one of her sisters living there, it allowed us to be closer to family while also helping Charity's career.

EXPANDING INFLUENCE

Charity is a natural influencer. She is wired to help people maximize their potential, live life to the fullest, do the things they have been called to do, and love well. Her heart beats to leave things better than she found them. The one tiny thing that Charity was feeling down about in Nashville was that only thirty to forty people were attending her *Money Wise* classes. She knew the value of what she was sharing and wished to help more people.

In agreement with what we felt God put on our hearts, our next dream was to expand Charity's influence while creating more free time for her. The only way she could increase her income from her salon was to work more hours; at this time in her life, that no longer aligned with her values. She wanted to create something that had room for financial growth but didn't place more demands on her time. She was hunting another unicorn. We had no idea what this was going to look like, but got everything on our end ready to move to Houston.

After sprucing up our house, we sold it—on our own—to our first prospective buyers during Thanksgiving week. Another miracle. It was so surreal, it felt like we were watching someone else's life unfold. Only God could orchestrate something that fast and hassle-free. The first week of January 2015, by plane, car, and moving truck, we left Nashville and headed south to Houston.

Within nine months of us moving to Houston, Charity published three books! I felt like I had to remind her there was no reason to push herself to write so much so fast, but she said, "I don't know why, but I know I am supposed to release these books now."

In hindsight, this rapid succession of books helped her develop a system of writing that would later be a large part of her dream. Over the next months, she connected with business coaches and developed a twelve-week coaching program to help other people become authors, too.

When Charity told me her idea, I had never heard of it before and wasn't even sure what she meant, but in true Charity style, she created something out of nothing. She started her own publishing company, LifeWise Books, which helps independent authors self-publish their books.

DREAMS DON'T COME EASILY

All of our dreams took a lot of hard work. Life was difficult at times. But in those challenging seasons, we experienced each other's strengths and weaknesses. We also saw that the world doesn't do your marriage any favors or take it easy on you. In fact, it seems as if the world is waiting for you to unravel and fall apart.

> AS A COUPLE, YOU MUST BOTH AGREE ON YOUR DREAMS AND THEN FIGHT FOR THEM.

As a couple, you must both agree on your dreams and then fight for them. Pursuing dreams is a joint effort when you're married, so once you've agreed, hold up your end and stay supportive. Prayerfully consider the full extent of what the dream will entail so you can ration your endurance, patience, and energy for the duration. If you're the one with the dream, be a finisher. Don't burn your spouse out on idea after idea you don't see to the finish line and then get mad when they don't want to support you on the next one.

Looking back, I am reminded of times when we took turns leaning on one another. Neither of us would be where we are today without the other. There is an equal amount of gratitude and appreciation for the belief and sacrifice we have each made to get here.

WHEN YOU'RE BETWEEN DREAMS

There may be times or long seasons when you or your spouse don't have a dream or vision for what's next in your life. It's a painful place to be. You know you don't want to stay where you're at, but you have no idea where to go or what to do. I remember times when I was just going through the motions at the warehouse like a robot. I wasn't particularly happy, nor was I particularly sad. I was just plugging along, but going nowhere.

That was an uncomfortable season for me. I was frustrated and underappreciated, which made me irritable. Charity listened intently for any signs of a plan from me to either adjust my attitude or move on to another job or some other situation that I felt held promise. Now, I realize the discomfort I was experiencing was the motivating factor for me to press in for direction from God. What did He have in mind when He made me? What interests did He give me? What experiences did I have in life that made an impact on me? What was I capable of? What would give me the feeling of being a contributing member of society?

This wasn't a short process, but it wasn't eternal either. I am thankful Charity stood by me through it. I know it was hard for her to watch as I didn't get an answer right away—or anything even close. Being the "practical-steps person" she is, she suggested we get help. We read books on changing careers, sought counsel, and invested in coaching. We gave the issue time and space, with lots of conversation and dream-talking. We also got deeply connected to our values. Charity's book, *Me, Myself & Why*, helps you identify your values so you can make decisions that flow with how you're wired and where you want to go.

Finally, when breakthrough came and the vision for my next season had clarity, we carefully and thoughtfully planned its course and began.

TO DO AND NOT TO DO LIST

If your spouse is between dreams or hasn't ever had one, I encourage you not to nag or pressure them. This method is unproductive and creates shame. In addition, jumping into something isn't likely to make them energized or happy. Instead, consider what you know about your spouse and be a contributing partner, helping them search for possibilities. Technology has made the world much smaller and easier to access. Information on careers based on personality, character, interests, and abilities is usually just a few filtered questions and searches away.

As a passionate multi-entrepreneur, Charity is always searching her soul. She's regularly asking, "What's the next step? Is what I'm doing now aligning with my values? How can I maximize my impact? Am I doing things that give me energy or drain it? Is what I'm doing still serving my family well?" She cross-checks her direction through filters like these. For her, changes may be incremental adjustments. But there have been several times when they were dramatic and life-changing.

Charity is very sensitive to impressions God gives her. When big changes and new dreams are churning, it usually starts with her having a gut feeling that transition is coming. This is not her favorite time; it's like finding out you're moving, but have no idea where you're going and you haven't even started to pack. At one point, Charity she said it felt like she needed to order business cards but had no idea what to put on them.

Outside of listening, praying with her, and helping her externally process her thoughts, there was nothing else I could do to ease the discomfort of her impending transition. We know now that if God had revealed everything all at once, we would likely have felt overwhelmed and said, "That's too much," and backed away from doing it. In His grace, this slow-play process of revelation allows us to accept the change in bite-sized portions.

TEAMWORK TO MAKE THE DREAM WORK

If your spouse has "taken one for the team" and sacrificed to help you get to your next level, take some time and help them reflect on what they see coming for themselves. Help draw out their latent potential and grow together. This may take more time than you can even fathom now.

What you can't see in the pages of this book are the years that went by while we were trying to figure this stuff out. It's easy to share about it and sum it up now, but those seasons and years of not knowing what was next were painful and required endurance.

The ultimate gift you can give one another is prayer and support coupled with practical wisdom and insight. If you remain a unified team, these transitional times feel less scary and more like the amazing opportunities they actually are. Charity and I have shared a couple of things that may help you at least get the conversation started either with your spouse or within yourself. As each of you becomes the "best you" together, you become the best team.

12

Grow and Strengthen Your Love

Charity

CELEBRATE YOUR STORY

One of the neatest gifts we were given when we got married was *The Book of Us*.[3] This is really a journal that asks you questions to coax the two of you to write your story. We have added to it over the years and it is heart-warming to go back through it and read what we wrote. We can recall where our love was at when we wrote our first few stories, what it was like when we added our

3. David and Kate Marshall, *The Book of Us: The Journal of Your Love Story in 150 Questions Diary* (New York, NY: Hyperion, 1998).

first child to the mix, and going through some hard things. It even contains all of the fluffy details of what we thought, felt, and did while dating. I love documenting this stuff because it allows us to remember where and how it all began.

CELEBRATING YOUR STORY PROVIDES FAR-REACHING BENEFITS.

Celebrating your story provides far-reaching benefits. Do yourselves a favor and begin writing it down. If you don't know where to start, here are some questions you can consider:

+ Who or what brought the two of you together?

+ How did you meet?

+ What were your thoughts when you first met?

+ What attracted you to your spouse?

+ What's your favorite feature about them?

+ How do they make you better?

+ How do you make them better?

+ What was the first brave thing you did as a couple?

+ What were some of your favorite trips together?

+ Whose feet are always cold?

+ Whose family is crazier? Why?

+ What was your biggest surprise about your spouse?

+ What do you love most about their character?

I hope these questions will inspire you and help you remember some of the beautiful initial details of your life and love together.

STRONG IS A JOURNEY, NOT A DESTINATION

As much as I would love to tell you that you can arrive at a strong marriage and then coast the rest of your lives, it's not true. Strength is a use-it-or-lose-it quality. While Ted and I may have years of great memories and history under our belts, we still have to live in the here and now with fresh love and commitment every day. The same is true for you.

What you did for your spouse years ago is great, but it can't be the only thing you have to talk about. Love grows or shrinks depending on the level of care it receives. To go the distance in marriage means you give your best today, you love your best today, and you commit your best today. Pledge to grow individually and together. Do what you can to not create pain in your marriage, but also know that a strong marriage doesn't equal a conflict-free marriage.

Strength is measured by the challenges it overcomes. What you've survived together speaks volumes about the strength in your marriage. As you navigate life after this book, I encourage you to revisit and write down the challenges your marriage has faced and how you made it through them. This is part of your story and again, it should be celebrated. If you are in the midst of a challenge, it will help you to recognize other situations that you've overcome. Allow past victories to build the faith needed for this one and the next.

PROTECT YOUR GROWING INVESTMENT

Be on guard for your marriage. Protect its gates—your eyes, ears, mind, and heart. What you see, hear, think about, and desire affect your relationship. There will likely be times when the heart wanders, even if only momentarily. This wandering is fed or starved by your thoughts and influences. If the media you consume or your friends talk about cheating like it's no big deal, you may soon find yourself agreeing. It's time to get off those websites, change channels, and find new friends.

> IF SEEN AND TREATED AS AN INVESTMENT, THE VALUE OF MARRIAGE GENERATES COMPOUND BENEFITS AND FAR SURPASSES THE SIMPLE ADDITION OF YOU PLUS ME.

In the heat of an argument, where does your mind go? Does it go to Splitsville or battle for togetherness? Draw the boundary lines on what your mind will entertain far away from the edge. Let reconciliation be the destination and desired outcome. Consider carefully the words you say and the thoughts you think.

Years of marriage are so much more than notches in a belt or hash marks marking the passage of time. They can either represent merely surviving or full-throttle thriving. If seen and treated as an investment, the value of marriage generates compound benefits and far surpasses the simple addition of you plus me.

SOMETHING TO LOOK FORWARD TO

One idea I heard from a friend really inspired me. She said she and her husband always have something on the calendar that they are looking forward to doing together. As you intentionally grow your love, let it include the hope and excitement of plans large or small. Whether it's a dinner out or a trip abroad, keep the home fires burning with plans for something you're doing together in the future.

Ted and I have poured our hearts and souls out on these pages. We hope we have given you lots of ideas and suggestions on how to set your marriage up to stay the course. What we don't

want to happen is for you to feel overwhelmed, not knowing where to
begin. Just pick one thing. You
can pick the biggest pain point,
the easiest attaboy, or something in between and work
it until you've got it ironed
out. Remember the person
you have the power to change
is you, so when picking, select
something you have the capacity
to work on.

> A STRONG MARRIAGE INVOLVES TWO STRONG PEOPLE, BUT THE STRONGEST MARRIAGES HAVE GOD AT THE CENTER.

ASK GOD FOR HELP

If you are at a loss and don't know what to do at this exact
moment, ask God, and then be still and listen. Let Him speak. My
experience is His voice isn't booming or loud. It's a quiet whisper
or impression I get in my heart and it usually touches on something I've been trying to avoid. Start where He leads you to start
and follow Him the rest of the way. A strong marriage involves
two strong people, but the strongest marriages have God at the
center.

A CLOSING NOTE FROM BOTH OF US

Friends, we hope this book encouraged and inspired you to
continue *Staying I Do* through whatever life brings. We are humbled by the opportunity to speak into your life and look forward
to hearing your story.

If you know of a marriage that's struggling, would you pass
this book on to them or get them a copy? It's in our heart to help

mend and reinforce marriages so couples can experience its beautiful divine design to the fullest.

Much love,
Charity & Ted Bradshaw

About the Authors

Ted and Charity Bradshaw both grew up in the area of Dallas/Fort Worth, Texas. As the children of multiple divorces, they decided they wanted something different than what they saw growing up. From the very beginning of their married life in 2002, they crafted healthy boundaries and open lines of communication that have allowed for honesty, love, and respect to flow freely. They have a passion for helping other couples build strong, loving, and fun marriages.

Charity is an author, business and writing coach, speaker, and president of LifeWise Books. She received a bachelor's degree in music from Oral Roberts University.

A registered nurse, Ted earned his Bachelor of Science degree in nursing from Middle Tennessee State University.

The Bradshaws reside in northwest Houston with their four children.

Index

Welcome to Our House!

We Have a Special Gift for You

It is our privilege and pleasure to share in your love of Christian books. We are committed to bringing you authors and books that feed, challenge, and enrich your faith.

To show our appreciation, we invite you to sign up to receive a specially selected **Reader Appreciation Gift**, with our compliments. Just go to the Web address at the bottom of this page.

God bless you as you seek a deeper walk with Him!

WE HAVE A GIFT FOR YOU. VISIT:

whpub.me/nonfictionthx

WHITAKER
HOUSE